Faculty Participation in Decision Making:
Necessity or Luxury?

by Carol Everly Floyd

ASHE-ERIC Higher Education Report No. 8, 1985

Prepared by

® *Clearinghouse on Higher Education*
The George Washington University

Published by

Association for the Study of Higher Education

Jonathan D. Fife,
Series Editor

Cite as

Floyd, Carol E. *Faculty Participation in Decision Making: Necessity or Luxury?* ASHE-ERIC Higher Education Report No. 8. Washington, D.C.: Association for the Study of Higher Education, 1985.

The ERIC Clearinghouse on Higher Education invites individuals to submit proposals for writing monographs for the Higher Education Report series. Proposals must include:
1. A detailed manuscript proposal of not more than five pages.
2. A 75-word summary to be used by several review committees for the initial screening and rating of each proposal.
3. A vita.
4. A writing sample.

Library of Congress Catalog Card Number 86-070251
ISSN 0884-0040
ISBN 0-913317-27-6

ERIC® **Clearinghouse on Higher Education**
The George Washington University
One Dupont Circle, Suite 630
Washington, D.C. 20036

ASHE Association for the Study of Higher Education
One Dupont Circle, Suite 630
Washington, D.C. 20036

This publication was partially prepared with funding from the National Institute of Education, U.S. Department of Education under contract no. 400-82-0011. The opinions expressed in this report do not necessarily reflect the positions or policies of NIE or the Department.

EXECUTIVE SUMMARY

Faculty participation in institutional decision making is accepted as intrinsically good and as having positive effects on institutional functioning, but it is reflected in varying degrees in actual practice. Neither faculty nor administrators have been very satisfied with the actual patterns of participation or the effectiveness of that participation. Faculty seek to protect and to reinvigorate historical mechanisms like academic senates and the well-established areas of curriculum and faculty tenure and promotion. They also seek mechanisms and approaches for establishing a significant role in areas where little participation historically has occurred. Sympathetic to faculty frustrations about participation, administrators seek ways to more fully integrate consultation with faculty into decision-making processes. Faculty and administrators are frustrated by the paucity of intrinsic and extrinsic satisfactions of faculty participation and seek ways to increase the rewards of that participation. Perceiving that many significant decisions are being made above the campus level, faculty now increasingly are concerned about mechanisms for participation at the system level in multicampus systems and at the state level.

What Is the Rationale for Faculty Participation in Institutional Decision Making?

The rationale for extensive faculty participation in institutional decision making rests on reasons for employees' participation in any organization and on reasons specific to the faculty role in higher education, the former contained in the sizable literature on generic organization theory and the latter in the more sparse higher education literature. Participation in institutional decision making is associated with increased employee satisfaction and performance in a wide variety of organizations. Employees' satisfaction and the quality of work life are now also increasingly viewed as valued outcomes in their own right. Faculty expertise on the subjects on which decisions are to be made is perhaps the most fundamental factor supporting faculty participation in institutional decision making. But faculty also tend to accord legitimacy to and fully cooperate in the implementation of only those policies that faculty have helped formulate because they believe faculty have a right to participate. Although participatory leadership models require

---

Faculty Participation in Decision Making

a number of preconditions, these preconditions are met in higher education environments more frequently than in other organizational settings.

How Do Academic Senates Serve as Effective Mechanisms for Faculty Participation in Campuswide Decision Making?
Faculty senates and faculty senate committees continue to be useful mechanisms for faculty participation at many research universities, at other universities, and at elite liberal arts colleges with regard to core academic areas like curriculum and faculty tenure and promotion, but they are not necessarily as influential at other types of higher education institutions. Senates are more representative of a cross-section of faculty in the 1980s than they were in the 1960s, the result of increased use of elected representatives and more democratic selecting procedures for committees. Faculty are less comfortable, however, with the involvement of nonfaculty constituencies in the revised senate structures established in the late 1960s and early 1970s and continue to seek means to minimize the influence of those constituencies. Collective bargaining has not significantly affected the functioning of coexisting senates in core academic areas on most campuses, but a number of factors are likely to lead to unstable senate/union relations in the future.

What Are the New Challenges to Faculty Participation and What Recent Developments Have Occurred Where Faculty Have Historically Not Participated?
Faculty historically have the broadest role and greatest influence on matters of curriculum and faculty personnel (especially tenure and promotion). The literature suggests, however, that these patterns may be difficult to maintain unless faculty are willing to address issues of general education, staffing flexibility, and some aspects of faculty conduct from a broader perspective. The resolution of these issues is central to faculty credibility and institutional viability.

Within the past 15 years, faculty participation has also become relatively well accepted in institutional planning and in the selection and evaluation of administrators at many institutions. Faculty participation is a significant element in the process by which presidents are selected and a normative factor against which presidential candidates are evaluated. Faculty ambivalence about integrating financial with academic factors, which has tended to restrict faculty participation and influence in some stages of planning, has also begun to recede. Healthy debates about the best mechanisms for integrating faculty participation into strategic planning suggest good prospects for balance between administrative leadership and broad participation as such approaches are actually implemented.

Although faculty involvement in budgeting and (in adverse circumstances) in retrenchment has historically been limited by both administrative resistance and faculty ambivalence, groundwork is being laid on many campuses for greater and more effective faculty participation. Faculty have begun to take steps, in conjunction with administrators, to gain a better understanding of the technical bases and political dynamics of the budgetary process, thus reducing an earlier handicap. Boards of trustees and university administrators are also becoming more sophisticated about the importance of process considerations in handling retrenchment and the greater acceptability of retrenchment measures if faculty are consulted about procedures and implementation.

What Steps Can Administrators Take to Integrate Faculty More Fully into Institutional Decision Making?

Administrators increasingly see themselves as managers of an institutional decision process and focus their energies on four crucial elements: strengthening the collegial foundations of decision making, shaping the consultative framework, increasing the availability of information, and facilitating group deliberation.

The articulation of a set of shared values and goals is central to strengthening the collegial foundations of decision making in higher education. In 1984 and 1985, a number of national blue ribbon commissions helped focus campus attention on the need to clarify the purposes of the undergraduate curriculum, with special emphasis on general education. Further, some scholars have suggested that Theory Z and other Japanese management approaches can help focus attention on a collegially oriented administrative style, while others have raised issues about some of the negative implications of Theory Z on the campus.

The higher education literature of the last 10 years reflects a growing consensus about the characteristics of and an adequate framework for administrative consultation with faculty. A set of understandings has evolved about where very broad consultation is useful and where the extent of consultation is appropriately more limited. Agreement has also been reached that every effort should be made to maintain process and procedure, even in crises.

Various approaches and means for administrators to make information relevant to campus-generated decisions more available to faculty consultative groups have been identified in the higher education literature. A national resource center for faculty participation in institutional decision making has been identified as a possible mechanism for providing a base of knowledge about best institutional practices.

Faculty and administrators can call upon a sizable literature on generic organization theory to gain useful insights to improve group deliberations. That literature illuminates various aspects of group decision making, including task-oriented leadership and group maintenance leadership, patterns of sharing group leadership, obstacles to rational evaluation of alternative decisions, and suggestions for improving group decision making.

What Steps Can Administrators and Faculty Take to Increase Faculty Satisfaction with Participation in Campuswide Decision Making?

The higher education literature contains a number of suggestions as to how institutions might increase the intrinsic satisfactions of and extrinsic rewards for institutional participation. Suggestions for increasing intrinsic satisfactions include providing faculty participants a better understanding of the dynamics of the consultative process and setting terms of committee service to correspond with the beginning and ending of major projects. Coordinated efforts of administrators and faculty are necessary to increase the extrinsic rewards for constructive institutional participation, thus reversing the pattern of very little weight given by most institutional personnel committees to institutional or public service, a pattern most accentuated in research universities.

What Are the Possible Alternate Mechanisms for Faculty Participation at the System Level and at the State Level?
Formal faculty participation at the system and state levels can take the form of direct membership on the board itself, a formal systemwide senate or statewide committee, or participation in ad hoc and standing technical committees. The mechanisms of a systemwide senate in multicampus systems or a statewide committee, such as a statewide coordinating board, have been of the strongest interest both in theory and in practice.

ADVISORY BOARD

CONSULTING EDITORS

Richard Alfred
Associate Professor and Chair
Graduate Program in Higher and Adult Continuing Education
University of Michigan

Robert Atwell
President
American Council on Education

Robert Barak
Deputy Executive Secretary
Director of Academic Affairs and Research
Iowa State Board of Regents

Larry Braskamp
Assistant to the Vice Chancellor for Academic Affairs
University of Illinois

Robert Cope
Professor of Higher Education
University of Washington

John W. Creswell
Associate Professor
Department of Educational Administration
University of Nebraska

Martin Finkelstein
Associate Professor of Higher Education Administration
Seton Hall University

Mary Frank Fox
Assistant Research Scientist
Center for Research on Social Organization
University of Michigan

Timothy Gallineau
Vice President for Student Development
Saint Bonaventure University

G. Manuel Gunne
Adjunct Associate Professor
College of Nursing
University of Utah

W. Lee Hansen
Professor
Department of Economics
University of Wisconsin

George Keller
Senior Vice President
Barton-Gillet Company

David W. Leslie
Professor and Chair
Department of Educational Leadership
The Florida State University

Gerald W. McLaughlin
Institutional Research and Planning Analysis
Virginia Polytechnic Institute and State University

Theodore J. Marchese
Vice President
American Association for Higher Education

L. Jackson Newell
Professor and Dean
University of Utah

Harold Orlans
Office of Programs and Policy
United States Civil Rights Commission

Patricia Rueckel
Executive Director
National Association for Women Deans,
    Administrators, and Counselors

Charles B. Saunders, Jr.
Vice President for Government Relations
American Council on Education

John E. Stecklein
Professor of Educational Psychology
University of Minnesota

Richard F. Stevens
Executive Director
National Association of Student Personnel Administrators

James H. Werntz, Jr.
Vice Chancellor for Academic Affairs
University of North Carolina

CONTENTS

FOREWORD

Is faculty participation in institutional decision making a necessity or a luxury? Making decisions, setting policies, and implementing procedures in a democratic fashion is a time-consuming process. Time is all too often viewed as a luxury, and often a luxury that appears to be unaffordable. Yet as Mortimer and Tierney explained in *Three "R's" of the Eighties: Reduction, Retrenchment, and Reallocation* (Report 4, 1979), there are times when an administrator must anticipate and make the luxury of time available for important decisions. For example, during the next decade such issues as an aging static faculty, continued retrenchment, faculty productivity, and posttenure evaluation are guaranteed to become crucial at nearly every institution. History has taught us that when issues arise that affect faculty, it is prudent to include faculty in the decision-making process. Administrators therefore should not wait for the inevitable crisis to make policies and procedures but should invite faculty to explore the problems now while time is more plentiful.

Is faculty participation desirable in setting everyday institutional policies and procedures? Yes. Employees must believe in the legitimacy of policies and procedures if they are to be implemented effectively and followed willingly. It is relevent to recall that faculty are trained and socialized to be highly independent professionals. The doctoral dissertation especially instills the value of independent scholarship: the tenure system likewise reinforces the independent nature of faculty activities. Faculty, then, are not the most complacent of employees, and not trained to succumb to autocratic administrators. The best way to instill confidence in administrative policies and procedures is to involve the employees in the process. Involvement builds commitment through personal ownership and encourages responsive behavior. For many faculty, it is imperative that they have a voice in the formative stage of policy-making to insure their loyalty in its implementation.

Active participation in policy-making will of course not guarantee total agreement. Second best, and preferred by some, is representative involvement, whereby designated members serve to advance the views of many. Within a college or university, representative involvement often takes the form of faculty senates, university committees, or other forums that develop and discuss ideas to make policy and procedural recommendations. These deliberative bodies may serve in an advisory capacity or as legislative agents, depending on the needs of the institution. Whatever form it takes, the need for faculty involvement in setting policies and procedures has ben demonstrated time and again, including in the earlier ASHE-ERIC Higher Education Report, *Flexibility in Academic Staffing: Effective Policies and Procedures,* (Report 1, 1985) and *Planning for Program Discontinuance: From Default to Design* (Report 5, 1982). An effective rule of thumb is the greater the faculty responsibility for the enforcement of a policy or procedure, the greater the need for faculty involvement in its development.

What is the legitimate role of the faculty in the institutional decision-making process? Carol Floyd, the director of Academic Planning and Program Review at the Illinois Board of Regents and adjunct associate professor of educational administration at Illinois State University, recognizes that different institutions will answer that question in different ways. Whereas a small, private college may prefer shared authority, a large, state institution may prefer separate jurisdictions for faculty and administrators. Dr. Floyd discusses the alternatives available for faculty participation not only on the institutional level but also within a larger system. Faculty can have an impact on the institution at all levels, be it in curriculum design, personnel status, or selection and evaluation of administrators.

This report, the final one in the 1985 series, will help administrators set a strategy for changing or implementing new policies. Recognizing that the morale of the faculty is vital to the success or failure of institutional goals is the first step to successful decision making.

Jonathan D. Fife
Series Editor
Professor and Director
ERIC Clearinghouse on Higher Education
The George Washington University

ACKNOWLEDGMENTS

I would like to acknowledge the help of Jonathan Fife, series editor, and the staff of the ERIC Clearinghouse on Higher Education for their assistance in preparing the monograph. Two outside reviewers also provided constructive comments that yielded useful insights for the final revision of the manuscript. I am grateful to Judy Hoffman for her help in typing the manuscript.

Finally, I am indebted to my husband, Steve, for all his help and encouragement.

INTRODUCTION

This monograph focuses on the literature related to participation by faculty in institutional decision making through
various mechanisms that have been established to provide
for an expression of faculty perspective and the integration
of that perspective into campuswide decision making. The
most frequently used mechanism of participation is a committee that is either connected with the campuswide academic senate or is directly advisory to campuswide administrators. Examination of faculty unions is limited here to
their impact on formalized faculty participation; the sizable
literature on faculty collective bargaining is outside the
scope of this monograph.

This monograph reviews the higher education literature
and the literature related to generic organization theory to
address various questions relating to faculty participation
in institutional decision making:

- *Rationale for faculty participation.* Does a strong
  rationale exist for employees' participation in some
  institutional decision making in any organization?
  What is the rationale for faculty participation in higher
  education decision making that is specific to the faculty role and to the higher education setting?
- *Alternate types of participation.* What are the differences in assumption and approach between images of
  faculty participation based on concepts of separate
  jurisdictions, shared authority, and joint participation?
  What are the strengths and weaknesses of each type?
- *Participation in academic senates.* What are the functions performed by academic senates? To what extent
  do faculty view academic senates as representative of
  the faculty viewpoint? What approach to decision
  making do senates typically use? What effect on academic senates do faculty unions have, and what effect
  can be anticipated in the future? How effective are
  academic senates?
- *Participation by functional area.* What are the historical patterns and current issues in areas like curriculum
  and faculty personnel where faculty have historically
  been the most active and influential participants?
  What participatory role has been established for faculty in administrative selection/evaluation and institutional planning? Is any headway being made in estab-

lishing a faculty role in areas like budgeting where the faculty role has historically been very small?

- *Participation at the system and state levels.* What mechanisms exist for faculty participation in decision making at these levels? What are the tradeoffs faculty must make as participants at these levels?

- *Participation and centralization/decentralization.* What are the implications of centralization and decentralization of institutional decision making for faculty opportunities to participate and upon overall attainment of institutional goals?

- *Strengthening consultative processes.* What can administrators do to strengthen the processes by which administrators consult with faculty in the decision-making process? What do the national blue ribbon commissions on higher education reform and Japanese management theory have to suggest about restoring collegial foundations for decision making? To what extent does a consensus exist about necessary elements of the consultative process? Where must consultation be broad and where can it justifiably be limited? What can campus administrators do to increase the information relevant to decision making available to faculty? How much information is available nationally on best institutional practice? What can faculty and administrators do to facilitate the deliberations of decision-making groups that include administrators and faculty?

- *Increasing faculty satisfaction with participation.* What are the sources of faculty ambivalence about participation in institutional decision making? Under what circumstances is it likely that faculty will resist participating in institutional decision making? What are typical problems with the intrinsic satisfactions and institutional rewards for participation and how might these problems be alleviated? What are the special problems for women and minorities regarding institutional incentives and disincentives for participation?

RATIONALE FOR FACULTY PARTICIPATION

The rationale for extensive faculty participation in institutional decision making rests on reasoning drawn from generic organization theory related to a broad range of organizations and on reasoning related more directly to the specifics of the faculty role in higher education. Drawing mostly on experience in a business setting, organization theory relates employees' participation in certain types of decision making with job satisfaction and job satisfaction with work productivity. The literature on faculty participation in institutional decision making is not as well developed as the literature drawing primarily on the business experience. It includes some application of organization theory to higher education but also contains other elements involving assumptions and analytical treatment of characteristics specific to higher education institutions.

The group where the change was made only after full participatory discussion was the most satisfied . . . and the most productive. . . .

Generic Organization Theory

The literature relating employees' participation and organizational productivity and functioning is substantial. Much of that literature relates to four aspects or links: relationships between participation, satisfaction, and performance; the relationship between leadership and participation; characteristics of the quality of work life; and the extent of employees' willingness to participate. The literature in the first two groups is more developed and has been subject to more review than literature in the latter two categories. A significant cataloging of the advantages and disadvantages of participation has also been developed.

Participation, satisfaction, and performance

One of the earliest and most frequently cited field experiments on the effects of participation was conducted in a garment factory to determine whether participation by sewing machine operators in designing new work procedures would reduce resistance to change in those procedures (Coch and French 1948). Two varieties of participation were compared to each other and to nonparticipation. The group where the change was made only after full participatory discussion was the most satisfied with the change and the most productive after the change was completely implemented (Coch and French 1948).

The overall pattern of the effect of participation upon satisfaction and performance is mixed with a more consistent pattern of effect upon satisfaction than upon performance. Many field experiments show no significant difference in effect between participatory approaches and nonparticipatory approaches, and in those cases where an impact exists, only about half show participation to have a positive effect (Lowin 1968; Yukl 1981, pp. 214–15). Taken together, the results of field experiments indicate that participation is more successful in some situations than in others and is more likely to improve employees' satisfaction than performance (Yukl 1981, p. 215). A similar pattern of mixed results has also been found in correlational field studies and laboratory studies, with satisfaction higher under participatory leadership but performance affected in no consistent manner (Locke and Schweiger 1979).

Methodological issues about the ways to conceptualize and measure participation and satisfaction have also arisen (Locke and Schweiger 1979; Mohr 1982; Sashkin 1984). Some quite fundamental questions have been raised about the nature of the questions asked of employees in many of the studies on participation. One critic believes that surveyed employees are not being asked to report the objective fact of participation but rather to express satisfaction with the degree of participation. He thus concludes that many studies have taken a misleading measure of participation, one that veers toward the reflection of satisfaction itself, and that therefore a partly spurious relationship is displayed (Mohr 1982, pp. 127–39). Another researcher concluded that improved goal setting or training rather than participation may account for some of the changes in productivity (Kanter 1983, pp. 271–72).

Suggestions to improve the methodology of participation literature include: (1) providing clearer definitions for participation and a more direct reference point for ''low participation''; (2) avoiding the assumption that if a positive relationship exists between participation and performance, then the more participation the better; (3) seeking to differentiate the effects of participation depending on the kind of issue; and (4) comparing the effect of different participation procedures (Yukl 1981, pp. 219–20).

Organizational theorists seek these methodological improvements because they find the relationship between participation and performance is highly situational and that the best approach to participation and leadership therefore depends on the circumstances (Kanter 1983; Vroom and Yetton 1973; Yukl 1981).

Situational theories of leadership and participation
Situational theories of the effectiveness of leadership are sometimes also called "contingency" theories, because they assume that the effect of leaders and leadership style on subordinates is contingent on situational variables. Situational variables include the nature of the task performed by the group, role expectations of superiors, peers, and subordinates, and the leader's authority to act (Yukl 1981, pp. 133–34). Major situational theories of leadership include Fiedler's contingency model (1967), Hersey and Blanchard's situational leadership theory (1977), House's path-goal theory of leadership (1971), and the Vroom-Yetton contingency model of leadership behavior (1973).

According to the Vroom-Yetton model, the leader must examine a number of aspects of a situation before determining the appropriate decision procedure (1973). These aspects include the importance of decision quality, the importance of decision acceptance, the amount of relevant information possessed by the leader and by subordinates, the likelihood that subordinates will accept an autocratic decision, the likelihood that subordinates will cooperate in trying to make a good decision if allowed to participate, and the amount of disagreement among subordinates with respect to the preferred alternatives. The model provides a set of rules for determining what decision procedures the leader should avoid in a given situation because decision quality or acceptance would be risked and identifies five possible levels of participation by subordinates to be chosen on the basis of the rules provided. For some situations, more than one level of participation by employees may be feasible. In this case, the choice as to the level of participation can be based on other considerations, such as time pressure, development of subordinates, and the leader's personal preferences (Vroom and Yetton 1973, chap. 3, 9).

The Vroom-Yetton model has been applied primarily in business settings and yields highly variable conclusions as to the appropriate amount of employees' participation parallel to wide variation in situational circumstances.

Quality of work life

A significant portion of the organization theory on the workplace has focused during the later 1970s and 1980s upon employees' satisfaction and the quality of work life as valued outcomes in their own right (Bobbitt and Behling 1981). The literature suggests that mature employees who are satisfied with a number of aspects of their working situation will also have a highly positive orientation toward work tasks and thus be highly productive employees (Cummings and Molloy 1977). Job enrichment is identified in the literature on quality of work life as one way to increase satisfaction in an employee group whose members have a strong need for personal growth (Perkins, Nieva, and Lawler 1983, p. 58). With increases in the educational level of the typical employee, greater percentages of the workforce are likely to have strong needs for personal growth. Increasingly, arguments for participation by employees are likely to emphasize its suitability for the workforce and work organizations rather than direct proofs of superior results (Lawler 1982).

Employees' willingness to participate

No universal willingness of employees to participate in making certain organizational decisions should be assumed to exist. Rather, employees are interested in and willing to participate in decisions that affect their own work units and their own jobs and are generally uninterested in participating in broader matters of policy. Some employees are more interested in participation than others. The employees most interested in participation are those who are highly interested in the task at hand and also interested in personal growth (Bass 1981, pp. 315–16; Kanter 1983, pp. 242–43, 252–54, 272).

Organizations have generally found that employees soon lose enthusiasm for or orientation toward participation in the absence of financial incentives or other formal rewards (Kanter 1983, pp. 255–56). Continued willingness to participate also depends upon employees' perceptions that advice given influences action taken. In the absence of that perception, the actions of organizational leaders will be regarded as manipulative and viewed in an entirely negative light (Kanter 1983, pp. 254–55; Wynn and Guditus 1984, p. 114). Communicating exactly what will or what will not come out of the process is a very important step toward minimizing possible disappointment (Kanter 1983, pp. 272–73).

Advantages and disadvantages of participation
Participation in organizational decision making can improve employees' satisfaction and performance in a number of ways:

1. Participation leads to greater understanding and acceptance of decisions.
2. Participation leads to greater identification with decisions and more intense commitment to their implementation.
3. Participation leads to greater understanding of objectives and action plans developed to achieve objectives.
4. Participation provides employees with a more accurate perception of organizational reward contingencies.
5. Participation is consistent with the needs of mature employees for self-identity, autonomy, achievement, and psychological growth.
6. When a decision arises from a participatory process, groups apply pressure on dissenters to accept or at least outwardly comply with decisions.
7. Group decision making promotes cooperation, mutual understanding, team identity, and coordination.
8. In cases of divergent objectives, consultation and joint decision making provide opportunities for resolving conflicts.
9. Participation allows the use of the expertise and analytical skills of individuals throughout the organization (Yukl 1981, pp. 208–9).

Participation also, however, entails certain disadvantages and limitations:

1. Broad participation is time consuming and not usable when an immediate decision is needed.
2. Decisions based on extremely broad participation may not give adequate weight to the primary applicable expertise.

---

3. Group decision making diffuses organizational responsibility, making it difficult to assign responsibility for success or blame for failure.
4. Providing for participation in some areas may lead to expectations for participation in a broader range of decisions than leaders may desire.
5. Extensive use of participation may result in a leader's being viewed as weak.
6. Participative decisions require special leadership skills and may lead to poor results if the leader lacks those skills (Yukl 1981, pp. 209–10).

Higher Education Literature
The rationale provided in the higher education literature for participation by faculty and influence in institutional decision making rests primarily on claims of a faculty right to participate and demonstration that faculty satisfaction and morale are closely related to opportunities for effective participation. Some very preliminary attention has also been given to the quality of work life and situational theories of leadership. Parallel to patterns found in other organizations, interest in participation focuses most clearly on and is most accepted within the basic departmental unit.

A right to participate
Faculty, more so than employees of other types of organizations, have claimed that participation in university decision making is inextricably bound with the institutional role of faculty and that faculty have what amounts to a right to participate.

As a right to participate in some significant fashion is assumed by faculty and not directly questioned by institutional administrators and boards of trustees, the bases for the claim to a right have been briefly noted in the literature, but no highly detailed rationale has been presented. Irving Spitzberg, for example, identifies the two primary bases for faculty participation in making significant institutional decisions: faculty expertise on the subjects on which decisions are to be made and a right to participate by those whose interests are at stake ("A Dialogue" 1983, p. 9). Two additional grounds are possible: (1) that those whose cooperation is essential to the effectiveness of a campus have the right to participate, and (2) that those whose efforts create and sustain institutional activity have the right to participate (Keeton 1971, chap. 1).

Participation, legitimacy, and satisfaction
The literature about higher education faculty suggests a relatively strong relationship between faculty participation and faculty satisfaction (Anderson 1983; Kamber 1984; Millett 1978; Mortimer, Gunne, and Leslie 1976). The most marked declines in faculty morale have been found at institutions where faculty perceive their role in institutional governance and planning has been significantly reduced (Anderson 1983). Faculty react in a strongly negative fashion to perceptions of a reduced role in institutional decision making because these perceptions suggest a totally distasteful image of faculty professional life and because they perceive such reductions to be a result of loss of administrative faith in the ability of faculty to help guide institutional affairs (Kamber 1984).

Faculty generally will not regard decisions as legitimately made if faculty have had no significant role in the making of those decisions, and, further, they are likely to resist the implementation of those decisions. A systematic study of eight community colleges, state colleges, and state universities, for example, compared levels of faculty participation in decision making with legitimacy of that decision making (Mortimer, Gunne, and Leslie 1976). On each campus, the legitimacy that faculty assigned to decision making in any given issue (including, for example, curriculum and merit raises) was closely related to the level of faculty participation in that area.

Of course, increases in the levels of faculty participation will not in every instance lead to increased faculty satisfaction. Increases in participation may lead to decreases in satisfaction if unrealistically high expectations are held of the results of that participation or if the participation becomes unduly burdensome (Helsabeck 1973, p. 58). It is also quite possible, however, that increased participation will result in lowered expectations as experienced participants become more realistic about the limits of organizational change (Cohen and March 1974).

Situational theories of leadership and participation in higher education

Applying the Vroom-Yetton model of leadership behavior to higher education would lead to a more frequent prescription of participative leadership styles than in other organizational settings (Vroom 1983). The relatively long time available for many higher education decisions would also permit the adoption of more participative processes. It is also likely that the situations a higher education leader faces will call for a range of leadership styles that range from a very high degree of employee participation to no employee participation (Vroom 1983).

The application of the factors in the Vroom-Yetton model in higher education settings frequently leads to the choice of depending heavily on faculty participation. University leaders are unlikely to possess all of the information necessary to make many decisions because of the high levels of specialization in a university. Problems are likely to be highly unstructured as a result of the lack of repetitiveness in the decisions that need to be made. Acceptance of decisions by faculty is usually crucial to effective implementation because formal control procedures are relatively absent and because faculty behavior is subject to low observability. Finally, the acceptability of an autocratic decision is likely to be low on any issue faculty have identified as important and about which opinions significantly differ (Vroom 1983).

Some statistically oriented studies, however, raise questions about the extent of the relationship between leadership approach and job satisfaction, as only small positive correlations have been found (Cope 1972; Wieland and Bachman 1966, both cited in Finkelstein 1984, pp. 145–46).

Quality of work life in higher education

Higher education scholars have recently suggested that the quality of work life perspective that has been developed primarily in business settings be applied to higher education. Higher education institutions should work toward the establishment of more explicit oganizational development approaches based on a modification of the organization theory and actual organizational practices developed in business settings (Bess 1983). The widely held assumption that it is important to ensure the quality of work life in the academic workplace and thus ensure the quality and productivity of the institution's instructional and other programmatic services makes it necessary to improve the quality of work life by providing additional opportunities for participation to strengthen faculty morale and organizational vitality (Austin and Gamson 1983). The findings of an empirically based national study of the conditions of faculty life in a broad range of institutions suggests that, in the mid-1980s, the satisfactions and frustrations of faculty life hang in an uneasy balance but that, in general, conditions seem to be improving at most research universities and liberal arts colleges (Bowen and Schuster *Forthcoming*).

Faculty satisfaction with departmental participation
The fact that faculty are concerned about autonomy and about participation has been frequently addressed in the literature (Austin and Gamson 1983, pp. 32–34). The primary means through which faculty have frequently sought influence, especially at research-oriented universities, is through establishing the departmental unit as a nearly autonomous unit.

Within the department, a decision-making structure and understandings are developed that provide for broad participation by all departmental members and for the leadership of the departmental chair. The typical departmental meeting and committee structure provides the primary opportunity for participation for most faculty members (Brown 1977; Tucker 1981). Of course, the departmental chair's approach to leadership varies according to the institution and the situation. Generally, faculty members are likely to express greater job satisfaction if they perceive their department chair's leadership style as being participatory (Finkelstein 1984, pp. 145–46).

Faculty members typically view effective and meaningful participation at the departmental level to be a major source of professional satisfaction, and they view departmental staff meetings as the most useful participatory device a higher education institution provides. Faculty most nearly achieve their conception of a group of independent professionals running their own affairs when they actively participate in a relatively autonomous departmental unit (Dykes 1968, p. 30).

Concluding Analysis

The rationale for extensive faculty participation in institutional decision making rests on the reasons for employees' participation in any organization plus additional reasons based on the specific character of the faculty role in higher education.

The generic organization theory provides an extensive catalog of reasons why participation in organizational decision making can improve employees' satisfaction and performance while also noting circumstances under which broad participation may be impossible or disadvantageous. This catalog is expanded for the higher education setting with the addition of the special role of participation in faculty members' image of their professional lives and their views of a right to participate. Faculty tend to accord little legitimacy to institutional decisions that appear to have been made with no faculty involvement and frequently resist the implementation of those policies.

Situational factors strongly affect the relationship between participation and performance; thus, the best approach to participation and leadership depends on the circumstances. Applying generic models of leadership behavior leads to a more frequent prescription of participative leadership styles in higher education than in other organizational settings because higher education problems are highly unstructured, because leaders do not have all the necessary information, and because acceptance of decisions by faculty is crucial to the effective implementation of decisions.

A significant portion of recent organization theory, whose insights are drawn primarily on business experience, has focused on employees' satisfaction and the quality of work life as valued outcomes in their own right. A similar literature on the higher education workplace has begun to develop.

The norm of separate jurisdictions for faculty and administrative decision making that was widely held during the 1950s and early 1960s was replaced during the late 1960s with norms typically described as "shared authority." This chapter describes the norms of separate jurisdictions and some of their limitations in practice and analyzes the concepts of shared authority as reflected in statements of blue ribbon commissions and study groups that examined the concept in the late 1960s and early 1970s. It also includes the concept of joint participation, which a number of analysts have offered in recent years as a useful modification of shared authority.

Separate Jurisdictions

The landmark study, *Governance of Colleges and Universities,* refers to a dualism of organizational structure involving differing structure and participants for making academic decisions than for making administrative (nonacademic) decisions (Corson 1960). Faculty play the central role in making decisions about educational matters, while administrators from outside academic areas make nonacademic decisions. Within academic areas, faculty are viewed as sharing fundamental premises about organizational purpose and process and as willing to receive new information and ideas and fully consider and discuss alternatives before reaching a consensus.

The concept of separate jurisdictions . . . views faculty as having a sphere of relatively independent action.

The concept of separate jurisdictions, which draws upon organizational dualism, views faculty as having a sphere of relatively independent action. Advocates of separate jurisdictions emphasize separate faculty deliberation and recommendations on all educational matters. Although no institution has operated fully under the concept of separate jurisdictions, some higher education faculties have operated with such concepts very much in mind. The primary example is the faculty of the University of California at Berkeley, which has totally embraced the concept of separate jurisdictions and has been regarded as having achieved an institutional role to be emulated by faculty at other research universities. The Berkeley faculty has fashioned the operation of its senate and related committees in a way that emphasizes separateness. The senate excludes administrators from membership or ex officio service on committees and does not regularly seek background information from university administrators. Any communication that has existed has been entirely informal and at best episodic (McConnell and Edelstein 1977; Mortimer and McConnell 1978, pp. 89–96).

At least two serious problems with the operation of a faculty governance system based on separate jurisdictions became apparent at Berkeley and similar institutions by the mid-1960s. First, the distinction between education and noneducational issues did not hold up well in practice. Second, the emphasis on separateness of jurisdictions discouraged attention to coordinating concerns of faculty and academic administrators (McConnell and Mortimer 1971).

The most obvious example of the lack of consensus over what was an educational issue arose when students disrupted campus activities to serve various political ends on issues external to the campus. When university administrators dealt with those disruptions directly as noneducational emergencies, faculty responded quite negatively, believing that such administrative actions against students had violated norms of the academic community and that the faculty should have a role in considering issues related to students' conduct. Although faculty and students by no means shared a fully common point of view, they agreed that matters of student conduct should not be a matter of administrative fiat (McConnell and Mortimer 1971). Putting aside issues of student conduct, it was becoming increasingly clear that many issues that were not strictly educational had educational consequences and that some faculty involvement in a broader area was desirable.

The lack of provision for direct coordination between faculty and academic administrators provided the basic ingredient for confrontation at the University of California at Berkeley when administrators received recommendations that they had no role in formulating and that may not have been examined at all with regard to feasibility (McConnell and Mortimer 1971, p. 175). Based on the analysis of a number of campuses, including Berkeley, "Separate faculty and administrative jurisdictions hinder mutual consultation, discourage administrative initiative, and provide little opportunity for persuasive leadership" (McConnell and Mortimer 1971, p. 177).

Shared Authority

Two major policy statements on academic governance
issued in the mid-1960s reflect the ideal that authority for
decision making should be shared among the constituencies of a higher education institution (American Association for Higher Education 1967; AAUP/ACE/AGB 1966).
The AAUP/ACE/AGB statement calls for a recognition of
the community of interest among the various parties—the
board of trustees, administration, faculty, students, and
other groups. It endorses the need for participation of faculty members, administrative officers, and governing
boards in determining "general education policy" and pro-
poses "joint endeavor" in selecting a president and
appointing other academic officers, in long-range planning,
in budgeting, in conducting external relations, and in preparing plans for physical facilities. Asserting that faculty
have primary responsibility for the curriculum, methods of
instruction, research, faculty status, degree requirements,
and some aspects of student life, the statement reaches two
conclusions with regard to joint effort: (1) The initiating
capacity and decision-making capabilities of all institutional components are needed in all important areas of
institutional decision making at one time or other, and (2)
the weight of the voice of each component should vary
from one issue to the next, depending upon the responsibility of the various parties for the particular matter at hand
(AAUP/ACE/AGB 1966).

Shared authority is equally central to the report of the
Task Force on Faculty Representation and Academic
Negotiation (American Association for Higher Education
1967). Reflecting its primarily faculty base, the report
makes some very specific recommendations to enhance the
faculty decision-making role and classifies the relative
extent of administrative and faculty participation in decision making along a five-zone continuum, with administrative dominance at one end and faculty dominance at the
other. The middle zone is termed the "shared authority"
zone, in which both faculty and administration exercise
"effective influence" on different issues. Under a system
of shared authority, the task force sees faculty and administration exercising a differential level of influence, depend-

ing on the nature of the matter at hand and suggesting that the means faculty use to assert influence will vary from campus to campus, depending on local circumstances. More specifically, the task force views delegation of decision-making authority to an academic senate and collective bargaining as varied kinds of shared authority having implications that would be quite different in a number of regards (American Association for Higher Education 1967).

Two other major reports about campus governance that stressed shared authority appeared in the early 1970s (Assembly on University Goals and Governance 1971; Carnegie Commission 1973). Emphasizing the importance of a division of authority among various groups, broad sharing of information, and a well-defined system of accountability, the report of the assembly maintained that "good governance depends on a reasonable allocation of responsibilities that makes the structure of authority credible for all groups" (Assembly 1971, p. 24). The report asserted that presidential leadership is quite important and that the presidential office should be strengthened to provide faculty leadership and to represent the overall interests of the university. It urged faculty members to give more attention to the work of faculty committees and faculty senates. And to ensure that academic administrators remain responsive to faculty perspectives, the report advocated a 12-year limit on administrative service (Assembly 1971).

The latter report, in its analysis of priority problems of higher education, included a significant treatment of the faculty role in governing board deliberations. The commission advocated faculty and student membership on appropriate board committees or, at the very minimum, an arrangement for joint consultation. Like the Assembly on University Goals and Governance, it asked that faculty from other institutions be considered for membership on governing boards. The commission also proposed that faculty members and students be involved in an advisory capacity in both the initial presidential appointment and in the review process following a term of presidential service (Carnegie Commission 1973).

Although a number of institutions and additional national commissions and committees issued reports in the late 1960s and early 1970s that embodied some significant aspects of concepts of shared authority (see Carnegie Commission 1973, app. C), none of the reports define precisely how authority should be shared. Such task forces and recommending groups have generally achieved consensus by avoiding highly specific statements; the strict sharing of authority works only in the absence of serious conflict (Richardson 1974). Statements on shared authority, however, even if not fully operationalizable, serve as important assertions that those affiliated with higher education institutions wish to emphasize that this approach should be used whenever possible (p. 349).

The normative statements presented in these reports provide a useful basis for understanding the general norms and preferences of the academic community with regard to the sharing of authority. They must also be regarded as having most of the shortcomings of the literature on academic and institutional governance. That literature has a number of problems (Hines and Hartmark 1980). It generally provides prescriptions that are operable only under ideal circumstances, limits itself to the formal apparatus of academic senates and their decisions, and provides little insight about the dynamics of campus political processes. It also provides little insight into patterns of conflict and consensus, about informal decision making, and about shifts in patterns of political dynamics (Hines and Hartmark 1980; O'Neil 1971).

The joint AAUP/ACE/AGB statement also has flaws: It is nondescriptive of practice at most institutions; it does not take into account adversary decision-making approaches inherent in collective bargaining for faculty; and it does not take into account relationships external to the campus (Mortimer and McConnell 1978, pp. 270–73). Shared authority was not the dominant pattern at most institutions in the mid-1970s, even on issues of most direct interest to faculty. Principles of shared governance were found to some extent at research universities, other universities, and a few selective liberal arts colleges but not at other types of institutions. And at some especially prestigious research universities, faculty seemed to prefer separate jurisdictions. Further, the 1966 statement did not directly address the subject of faculty relations with system-level and state-level authorities (Mortimer and McConnell 1978).

Joint Participation

Much of the literature of the last 10 years focuses less on the specifics of how authority is to be shared and more on new approaches for encouraging joint participation of faculty and administrators, with special emphasis on extensive administrative consultation with faculty over the broad range of institutional decisions. What is needed, for example, is ". . . well-established procedures that guarantee constituents effective roles in decision making and implementation" (Powers and Powers 1983, p. 3). An approach that emphasizes joint participation both provides campus constituencies a greater role in decision making and preserves essential hierarchies (p. 4). In a joint participation approach, faculty and administrators share other things than authority: the opportunity to participate, the information necessary to participate effectively, access to decision makers, an opportunity to influence decisions, the responsibility to develop a perspective broader than narrowly defined individual or group self-interest, and the responsibility to take at least some of the advice received (Newman and Mortimer 1985).

In contrast to the concepts of separate jurisdiction and shared authority, which assert that one group or another has the primary interest on a particular subject, joint participation more explicitly recognizes the legitimate interests of a number of groups (Mortimer and McConnell 1978, p. 270; Powers and Powers 1983, pp. 3–4). In joint participation, codification of the historical faculty role is also regarded as possibly deleterious to a strong faculty stance for two overlapping but different reasons. First, such codification may hamper the broad potential influence of faculty, as no listing can be all-inclusive, and if not listed, an area is likely to be considered under implied administrative jurisdiction (Powers and Powers 1983, pp. 120–21). Second, faculty increasingly realize that they now wish to participate in a number of decision areas (the most notable of which is budgetary and financial) where faculty have historically not been active or asserted a major role and that joint participation is therefore desirable (Mortimer and McConnell 1978, p. 271).

Proponents of joint participation view strong administrative leadership as not only consistent with broad faculty participation in institutional decision making but also necessary for providing the framework and environment in which that participation can be most effective (Mortimer and McConnell 1978; Powers and Powers 1983). Strong institutional leadership is needed for administrators and faculty to work jointly toward clearer definitions of and attainment of institutional goals.

Concluding Analysis

Alternate types of faculty participation in institutional decision making are separate jurisdictions, shared authority, and joint participation. In the case of separate jurisdictions, faculty are viewed as having a sphere of relatively independent action on educational issues. Although faculty at a few major research universities hold these concepts as ideal, no institution fully operates under such understandings, and recent higher education literature only rarely makes use of such concepts.

Concepts of shared authority stress that faculty and administrators should share authority in most areas, with primary responsibility varying depending on the subject area. Although such statements provide a useful basis for understanding the general preferences of the academic community, they are now generally regarded as workable only in the absence of significant conflict. In the 1980s, writers avoid specifying the distribution of authority among the parties, thus assigning shared authority roughly the same meaning as joint participation.

Joint participation focuses less on the specifics of how authority is to be shared and more on approaches for encouraging the joint participation of faculty and administrators over the broad range of institutional decisions. Its primary strengths are its avoidance of too narrow a codification of the areas of faculty involvement and its explicit recognition of the interests of other campus constituencies. The primary source of faculty discomfort with this type of participation is its explicit recognition of the necessity of organizational hierarchy.

Most higher education institutions have an academic senate in which faculty members hold a majority of the seats and that is intended to serve, as a whole and through its committees, a number of significant legislative, advisory, or forensic functions (Mortimer and McConnell 1978). In a few areas, the most notable of which is curriculum, senates have quasi-formal authority. Senate authority on most issues is the functional authority of providing advice to the university administration with the expectation that reasons will be given when administrative officers take a course of action different from that advised by the senate. Finally, senates provide an opportunity for the public discussion of a wide range of issues important to the academic community but on which no immediate institutional decision must be reached (Mortimer and McConnell 1978, pp. 27–30).

During the late 1960s and early 1970s, faculty pushed hard to strengthen the academic senate as an avenue for influence on institutional policy. The report of the Task Force on Faculty Representation and Academic Negotiation gave the greatest visibility to that faculty initiative. It advocated shared authority between faculty and administrators to be exercised primarily through an academic senate in which faculty members would constitute a clear majority (American Association for Higher Education 1967). During that period, attention was also focused on mechanisms for students' participation in university decision making and the extremely divisive issues raised by social upheaval in general and disruptive student behavior on campus in particular (Millett 1978). Optimism that a stronger academic senate was the key to greater faculty participation and more effective faculty influence was relatively widespread during that period.

Analysis and evaluation of the extent to which academic senates have been a useful mechanism for faculty participation and influence were significant elements of the literature on faculty senates during the 1960s and 1970s and became even more prominent in the mid-1970s, as extreme optimism about the potential of senates began to wane. Aspects of concern about academic senates can be grouped into five broad categories: (1) representativeness of faculty, (2) clarity of the voice of faculty separate from that of other campus constituencies, (3) decision-making approach

Senate authority on most issues is the functional authority of providing advice to the university administration.

and style, (4) viability in collective bargaining, and (5) overall effectiveness.

Representativeness of Faculty
The faculty as a whole will view decisions made by academic senates as legitimate only if the senate is viewed as including a representative cross-section of institutional faculty (Mortimer and McConnell 1978). Among the criteria for representativeness are eligibility for membership, structure of the senate, and patterns of committee service (p. 31).

The basic definition of "faculty" varies from institution to institution. On one hand, some institutions include nearly all instructional faculty and academic professionals. Others, mostly research universities, limit eligibility for the senate to ranked tenure-track or tenured faculty. The former definition provides a broader base of campus legitimacy, but the latter definition probably fosters a more cohesive sense of faculty identity (Mortimer and McConnell 1978, pp. 31–32).

Senates use a variety of structural arrangements (Mason 1972). Some are structured as town meetings, others as elected bodies of representatives. The town meeting has been and continues to be the typical structure for senates of small institutions. Although the rationale for a representative body is quite strong at larger institutions—the result of the size of the faculty and the complexity of senate affairs—some large public research universities (the University of California at Berkeley and the University of Wisconsin at Madison, for example) retained a town meeting form of senate until the early 1970s. The retention of that format at those institutions clearly underlines the appeal of the town meeting even in the largest and most complex institutions because of the strong current in faculty culture emphasizing the involvement of the individual faculty member in institutional decision making (Mortimer and McConnell 1978, pp. 32–36).

As a result of problems encountered with the town meeting form, town meeting senates had been transformed into elected bodies at most institutions except very small liberal arts colleges by the mid-1970s. Town meetings were viewed as easy for a small minority to manipulate, as generating unusual hostility between factions, and as providing an environment encouraging to faculty "showmen" but discouraging to many faculty representing the most "humane" values (Mortimer and McConnell 1978, p. 36).

A related question concerns committee service and whether it is concentrated in the hands of a few activists. A review of a number of analyses of committee configurations at various campuses during the early 1970s, found that committee service at many institutions was concentrated by rank, sex, and academic discipline (Mortimer and McConnell 1978). The young, women, and minorities rarely served on significant committees, suggesting that those patterns of concentration of committee service seem connected with informal patterns of selection of committee members and hence the need for more systematic selection (pp. 36–39). In fact, during the late 1970s and early 1980s, committee service has become significantly less concentrated at many institutions.

Voice of Faculty
Issues about the extent to which senates are constructed in a fashion to provide a clear faculty voice have evolved as changes have occurred in senate membership bases. In an earlier period when most senates included only faculty, the major issue on many campuses was the extent to which administrators should participate in senate affairs. The opposition to administrative involvement in senate committees emphasized the need for a pure faculty voice on matters of primary interest to faculty. Supporters of direct administrative involvement in academic senate committees pointed out that in the absence of such involvement little administrative commitment to carry out decisions is likely, and "Joint deliberation, negotiation, and shared decision making are preferable to disjunctive and adversarial relations" (McConnell and Mortimer 1971, p. 50).

During the 1970s, faculty started to express concerns about whether broadening the membership base to include additional campus constituencies had led to a diminution of the faculty voice on issues of primary faculty interest. The most specific complaints focused on student and other non-faculty involvement in the areas of curriculum and faculty tenure and promotion, accepted at most institutions as areas of strong faculty authority (Millett 1978, p. 225). Recently, sentiment has grown on some campuses for a configuration that provides a senate to each major campus constituency, which could then deliberate for itself within its own senate. Provision would also be made for some institutional mechanism for debating issues between constituencies (Spitzberg 1984, p. 17a).

Faculty are likely to give continuing attention to constructing senates so as to provide for clearer expression of the faculty voice. Although faculty at some institutions may attempt to return the senate to a narrower base (Meyer 1985), the formal institutional rejection of a broadly based senate is unlikely to occur at many institutions in the foreseeable future. Faculty are therefore likely to seek other alternatives, including that of a faculty caucus within the institutional senate that meets regularly to deliberate on issues of primary interest to faculty.

Decision-Making Orientation
Commentators on the decision-making processes of academic senates express concerns about maintaining vigorous debate and approaching decision making primarily on a consensual basis. Proceeding on the basis of direct observation of senate patterns and on reviews of the literature, observers note difficulties likely to arise in the first regard when an academic senate has a large number of members. If a large senate wants to do useful work, it needs to divide itself into a number of internal task forces (Hodgkinson 1974, p. 140). Although senates must be large enough to keep them from being monopolized by a single faction, they must be small enough to permit vigorous debate on substantive issues (McConnell and Mortimer 1971, p. 166).

Failures to achieve consensus in senate practice have been described and explained in a variety of ways. During the early and mid-1970s, shortcomings were described primarily in terms of overt politicization and extreme factionalism (Balderston 1974, p. 86; Mortimer and McConnell 1978, p. 268). More recently, commentators have focused on voting in faculty decision-making bodies as central to the deficiency (Nichols 1982b, p. 8; Powers and Powers 1983). A style emphasizing voting fosters an environment where decisions are made by narrow majorities, leaving substantial minorities of the faculty strongly dissatisfied (Nichols 1982b, p. 8). Others caution, however, that a lack of full consensus should not be equated with lack of consultation or attempts at reaching consensus, as higher education institutions have historically sought to accommodate diversity within a broad consensual framework (Chait 1982b).

Collective Bargaining Setting

The impact of collective bargaining on the functioning of academic senates is the major focus of that portion of the literature on unionization that deals with matters other than wages, hours, and working conditions. The literature identifies models of union/senate interaction, actual practices categorized in terms of those models, advantages and disadvantages of contractualizing the status of senates, and sources of stability and instability in the current dominant pattern of relationship.

Three models of union/senate interaction have been identified: the cooperative model, the competitive model, and the cooptative model. In the cooperative model (sometimes referred to as the dual-track model), both union and senate retain their independence and control their own jurisdictions with little interference. In the competitive model, the union and senate compete for support of faculty and for the right to control decisions over major issues. In the cooptative model, the senate ceases to exist as a senate and is either folded into the union or abolished (Garbarino 1975, pp. 145–49).

The cooperative or dual-track model has been identified as the dominant model in practice for institutions having single campus bargaining units. Differentiation of the two tracks has been clearest at institutions where the academic senate was strong before collective bargaining and where intracampus conflict within the faculty and with administrators is relatively low (Mortimer and McConnell 1978, pp. 84–85). Academic senates have concentrated on matters of basic academic policy and have historically not been involved in questions of wages, hours, and working conditions. On those few campuses where senates had been involved in employment questions before unionization, senates withdrew from involvement after the selection of a collective bargaining agent. Unions frequently have not sought involvement in the areas of traditional senate concentration because they saw no advantage in doing so (Baldridge, Kemerer, and associates 1981; Johnstone

1981; Lee 1978; Mortimer and Richardson 1977).

Although faculty unions have frequently been concerned about maintaining the academic senate, that concern has not typically been directly reflected in collective bargaining agreements because of the union belief that collegial governance traditions depend heavily on an informal delegation of powers by trustees and administration and that a request to formalize would probably engender a strong trustee and administrative impulse to reserve as much power as possible. Some leaders of faculty unions still argue, however, that the position of the faculty senate should be protected by specific provisions in state collective bargaining laws or in the negotiated collective bargaining contract ("Four Issues" 1982, pp. 9A–11A).

Factors providing some stability to a dual-track model during the 1970s were faculty and union preferences, administrative preferences, and a legal environment restricting the scope of bargaining (Baldridge, Kemerer, and associates 1981; Lee 1978; Mortimer and Richardson 1977). The Carnegie Council, especially, favored limiting the scope of bargaining to economic issues and securing statutory provisions protecting collegial decision areas (1977). On the other hand, certain factors tend to increase competition between the academic senate and the collective bargaining agent: a high level of intrafaculty conflict and a bargaining unit broader than ranked tenured and tenure-track faculty (Mortimer and McConnel 1978, pp. 84–85).

Although observing a relatively stable dual-track system on most campuses during the 1970s, most analysts identified factors that are likely to contribute to instability in senate/union relations by the late 1980s. Observed increases in conflict in the external environment of higher education are likely to add new strains to internal relationships (Baldridge, Kemerer, and associates 1981, p. 8). A number of forces will also tend to broaden the scope of bargaining and thus bring unions into areas where academic senates have traditionally been involved. The scope of bargaining is likely to broaden on the basis of case-by-case interpretations of legal restrictions and as a response to the realities of bargaining relationships (Begin 1978). As the scope of bargaining has broadened after about 10 years in other professions that have experience with collective bargaining, such broadening may well begin to occur at a number of higher education institutions in the near future (Clark 1981). In a period when economic concessions are not forthcoming, unions are likely to seek new areas in which to gain new benefits for their members but will have difficulty in finding new areas that do not involve making painful decisions (Kemerer and Baldridge 1981). Although unions have frequently regarded retrenchment as a painful decision area to be avoided, they have more recently become more directly involved, to the frustration of academic senates (Jacobsen 1984).

On the whole, the literature on collective bargaining in higher education that analyzes the experience of the 1970s suggests that academic senates that were viable before collective bargaining have usually also been viable since the advent of collective bargaining. In light of the likelihood of an increasingly broad scope of collective bargaining on many campuses in the future, competition between academic senates and collective bargaining agents may well increase to the serious disadvantage of academic senates. The continued existence of the dual-track model on most campuses depends on the extent to which unions find utility in the continued existence of senates and senate involvement on various topics rather than to the strength of the academic senate in dealing with union opposition (Lee 1978, pp. 28–29).

Overall Effectiveness
A reasonable evaluation of the effectiveness of academic senates is based on the extent to which senates and senate committees are influential on matters on which they spend the greatest portion of their time. The primary focus of senates has been core academic policy and the protection of a significant extent of departmental autonomy (Angell 1978; Johnson and Mortimer 1977; Lee 1978).

Two reports on studies of the faculty role and senate influence at selected institutions in the early and middle 1970s use different research methodology, employ different institutional taxonomies, and include somewhat different research findings. The first is based on a major research project conducted at the Stanford Center for Research and Development in Teaching (Baldridge et al. 1978). The second is based on a set of case studies prepared by campus-based analysts; the overall framework and subsequent analysis were provided by the study director (Millett 1978). Both studies differentiate between faculty influence and the senate mechanism as one possible mechanism for that influence, and both conclude that faculty are quite influential at major research universities. In one study, that influence was primarily in academic departments with a moderately strong senate dealing with the very limited number of academic matters that are actually left for resolution at the institutional level (Baldridge et al. 1978). Millett found strong faculty influence at other universities with well-established graduate missions but a lesser research orientation. Baldridge et al. found the highest levels of faculty participation in campus governance and the strongest academic senates at elite liberal arts colleges, where faculty participated actively in departments and in the institutional senate. Both studies found relatively weak faculty participation and weak senates at nonelite private liberal arts colleges and at public comprehensive institutions and public colleges. Most of the latter were of relatively recent origin or in the midst of transformation from teachers colleges. Little faculty participation and weak or nonexistent senates were the rule at most community colleges (Baldridge et al. 1978).

As few empirically based studies of institutional governance and senates have been conducted since the mid-1970s, little basis exists to test these conclusions in light of more recent developments at a relatively broad range of institutions. One recent examination suggests, however, that the role of faculty was enhanced rather than diminished during the 1970s at a significant number of nonelite liberal arts colleges (Finkelstein and Pfinister 1984).

Concluding Analysis
Faculty senates and their committee structures continue to be a useful mechanism for campuswide faculty participation at research universities, other universities with well-established graduate missions, and elite liberal arts colleges on core academic areas like curriculum and faculty tenure and promotion. They would appear to be less influential at other types of higher education institutions.

Senates at larger institutions reflect a more representative cross-section of faculty in the 1980s than they did in the 1960s, because the elected representative format has replaced the town meeting format and because committee assignments now include greater numbers of junior faculty, minorities, and women. Faculty remain uncomfortable about the involvement of nonfaculty constituencies in deliberations on many academic matters and are likely to seek mechanisms and approaches that minimize that influence. Tensions between consensual norms and rule of the majority for decision making continue to be noticeable in senates as well as in other decisional settings on some campuses. Collective bargaining has had little effect on coexisting senates in the academic areas of primary senate influence but has excluded any previous limited senate involvement on matters of wages, hours, and working conditions. Union/senate relations are likely to be more unstable in the future as the result of external strains on institutions and the broader scope of bargaining ordinarily associated with the maturing of a collective bargaining relationship.

A substantial portion of the literature on faculty participation focuses on that participation in one particular functional area of university decision making. This chapter reviews that literature with emphasis on patterns and range of institutional practice, effect of participation, faculty satisfaction and dissatisfaction, and experience with or suggestions for new approaches. The first two functional areas examined (curriculum design and faculty personnel status) are areas where faculty historically have been very active and influential participants. The other areas include selection and evaluation of university administrators, planning (including strategic planning), budgeting, and the special case of planning for retrenchment (as well as financial exigency).

Curriculum Design

Faculty participation in determining the institutional curriculum has deep historical roots; in most institutions, faculty either control the curriculum or are the strongest influence upon it (Levine 1978; Millett 1978). Faculty exercise primary influence in several curricular areas: establishment of new degree requirements, development of courses satisfying those requirements, and development of course objectives and course content (Millett 1978). The related areas of instructional procedure and evaluation of students' learning achievements are also primarily under faculty influence (p. 28). The area of curriculum is the area of greatest historic strength of campuswide senates. The academic senate, typically through a curriculum committee, has exercised legislative or quasi-legislative authority over the major curricular processes like the approval of new courses (McConnell and Mortimer 1971, pp. 123–25).

Many faculty members and administrators have been frustrated during the 1970s and 1980s by difficulties in winning support for curricular change. Although a substantial portion of institutional faculty strongly believe that the curriculum needs significant change, faculty are also identified as the primary barrier to change because of inertia caused by disciplinary orientation, internal divisions, and a process that accords them veto power (Levine 1978, p. 425).

Increased interest in the function of and administrative leadership provided curriculum committees has resulted from strong desires to reformulate and reinvigorate the

. . . Faculty are also identified as the primary barrier to change because of inertia caused by disciplinary orientation, internal divisions, and . . . veto power.

general education portion of the undergraduate curriculum. Clark Kerr, for example, emphasizes the importance of vigorous administrative leadership, especially at the presidential level, as he believes that the faculty is not the primary constituency for liberal learning (1984). The recent reinvigoration of general education at a number of institutions shows that faculty committees have acted constructively, if not necessarily taking the initiative (Spitzberg 1984). Faculty must act responsibly and take further initiatives with regard to the curriculum, and they must be extremely restrained in the use of their effective veto on curriculum matters (p. 18a).

Faculty Personnel Status
Faculty at most institutions participate in making decisions on the most significant matters relating to faculty status, assisting in recruiting new faculty members; approving backgrounds of candidates for appointment; setting faculty performance standards and participating within their disciplines in peer review on matters of tenure, promotion, and dismissal; and sitting on committees to hear faculty grievances (Fortunato and Waddell 1981, p. 9). Such activities are the operation of the concept of faculty responsibility for determining its own membership. The extent of acceptance and operation of the concept varies a great deal, depending on institutional mission, level of institutional maturity, sources of support, and legal status and history (Commission on Academic Tenure 1973, chap. 1; Smith 1978).

The organizing concepts and structures underlying the policies and procedures of the most mature and comprehensive universities include peer selection and review, the principle of merit, the principle of tenure, a set of checks, balances, and constraints, and a climate of consultation (Smith 1978, pp. 5–10). The faculty and administration must address certain faculty personnel issues if the integrity of the tenure system is to be maintained: (1) tenure density and the inflexible base of faculty expertise; (2) balancing the claims of society, the institution, and the college versus claims of the department and individual faculty members; and (3) increased codification resulting from increasing external intervention. Faculty must work with administrators to find some level of institutional flexibility in the assignment of resources while continuing strong support of the tenure system. A carelessly drawn procedure for dealing with the inflexibility of the tenure system in highly tenured units would probably lead to the same consequences that would flow from simple abandonment of the tenure system (Smith 1978, pp. 10–13).

The Keast Commission, which was sponsored by the American Association of University Professors and the Association of American Colleges, proposed campus staff plans as a way to retain both tenure and flexibility. Such rolling plans should be prepared and reviewed annually and should be developed through joint faculty/administration consultation (Commission on Academic Tenure 1973, p. 47). Although such staff plans have not been widely adopted, a variation of the concept was successful in the Illinois Regency Universities System, where the "plans" were used as a reporting and predicting instrument (Groves 1981). The "plans" have met many of the expectations of the Board of Regents, but extensive consultation between faculty and administrators at all levels has failed to materialize. Faculty have not seriously contested the lack of a significant consultative role, probably because of some faculty discomfort with participation in this activity as well as the lack of secrecy and implementation force of the plans (Groves 1981).

Faculty members have a long-standing and well-established role in appellate procedures relating to peer review in the processes for appointment, promotion, and awarding of tenure. The grievances of faculty members are frequently handled by an appeals panel or mediator drawn from the faculty. Wide consultation with a broadly based group of faculty is regarded as especially important when developing campuswide statements on responsibility, due process, and rights to appeal (Powers and Powers 1983, pp. 97–103).

Collective bargaining has not resulted, at most institutions, in major changes in approaches to or procedures for tenure. Faculty personnel decisions are generally handled by a faculty committee separate from both the union and the senate (Lee 1982, pp. 80–81). Although formal grievances filed under collective bargaining contracts do not appear to have reduced faculty participation in academic decision making, arbitrary decisions have sometimes posed problems for traditions of academic peer evaluation, as it is difficult for arbitrators to separate procedural judgment from substantive judgment (Lee 1978, pp. 37–38). One way of preventing interference with peer judgment is to specify carefully the remedial powers of arbitrators (Weisberger 1978, p. 7). As arbitrators become more experienced in hearing and evaluating higher education grievances, they may also become more familiar with characteristics of academic decision processes and may improve their abilities to distinguish between procedural and substantive academic issues (Lee 1978, pp. 37–38).

As a result of external pressures, faculty personnel policies have broadened in scope from a relatively sparse formulation of tenure and promotion requirements to a broader set of regulations that also restrict faculty conduct in certain regards. Many institutions have recently adopted or are currently formulating regulations for areas like outside consulting, patents and copyrights, possible conflicts of interest, allegations of fraud in research, professional ethics, and faculty/student interaction (including the prevention of sexual harassment). Assertions of a strong faculty role in institutional policy making in this area are now beginning to appear in the higher education literature. For example, joint deliberation by faculty and administration is essential to the resolution of issues on regulation of faculty conduct in a manner that minimizes the effect on the higher education workplace as well as faculty resentment and dissatisfaction (Olswang and Lee 1984).

Selection and Evaluation of Administrators
The rationale for faculty participation in the selection and evaluation of administrators—especially deans, academic vice presidents, and presidents—has been frequently stated (Farmer 1978; Strohm 1980). Many faculty and administrators support representative search and selection committees as the best means of ensuring appropriate faculty participation in the selection of academic affairs administrators. Some attention has also been given to procedures to provide an information flow from the faculty to the committee members in the form of opinions or preferences. In one instance, the faculty of a business school's expressed preferences for a dean's role were identified through small group discussions and the administration of a

questionnaire (Pollay, Taylor, and Thompson 1976). The approach not only increased faculty influence on the selection process but also set the political groundwork to ensure a greater faculty role during the new dean's tenure in office (Pollay, Taylor, and Thompson 1976).

The faculty's role in the selection of the president or other chief executive become relatively well established during the 1970s. By the late 1970s, over two-thirds of the search and selection committees of higher education institutions included faculty, with public institutions more likely to include faculty on such committees than private institutions (Nason 1981, p. 121). A single heterogenous search committee is more advantageous in two ways than a board committee advised by separate committees for each major campus constituency: First, months of working together generate a sense of common purpose, and second, the new president starts service with the support of the various campus constituencies (Nason 1981, p. 121). Members of the board of trustees generally regard faculty as making an essential contribution to the presidential search committee but as making little contribution to the broader discussion frequently occurring in conjunction with presidential selection about subjects like the possibility of the institution's increasing its service to additional clienteles, such as part-time adult students. Trustees have also noted some special difficulties when candidates are from inside the institution. Faculty have occasionally been hesitant to comment on an internal candidate but have also waged personal campaigns against other internal candidates (Robinson 1982). The commitment of presidential candidates to faculty participation and their ability to manage the process of consulting faculty and other campus constituencies has also become a major factor in presidential selection (Powers and Powers 1984).

Although the principle that the perspectives of faculty on the performance of presidential incumbents should be considered in the review process is well accepted at many institutions (Nason 1980), practices on how those perspectives should be ascertained as well as other characteristics of the review process for incumbent presidents are somewhat unsettled. The Commission on Strengthening Presidential Leadership (sponsored by the Association of Governing Boards and funded by the Carnegie Corporation) focused on terms and conditions of the presidential position that strain many incumbents and inhibit the recruitment and retention of able administrative leaders (1984). Noting problems of confidentiality in some past evaluations, trustees are currently inclined toward evaluation methods that preserve the privacy of the incumbent and do not encourage open attack. Trustees see their ends as best achieved by reviews conducted annually and informally that involve the solicitation of the opinions of those faculty who have direct and regular contact with the president.

Planning (Including Strategic Planning)

During the 1960s, faculty were not very interested in participating in institutional planning because such activity was typically quantitatively oriented and did not seem to have any significant effect on educational policy (Palola, Lehmann, and Blischke 1971). During the 1970s and 1980s, however, planning has been seen as having a direct impact on educational policy, and both administrators and faculty have sought appropriate means to ensure that planning will benefit from faculty insights and perspectives (Haas 1980).

The degree of faculty participation has varied according to the type of planning involved, with faculty participation greatest in activity focusing on academic programming, especially on review of degree programs (Poulton 1980). Limiting factors on faculty participation in planning above the departmental level are shortage of time, complexities of the task, and the lack of rewards (Poulton 1980).

During the late 1970s and the 1980s, institutionwide faculty committees have been heavily involved in the review of proposals for new degree programs and in regular periodic review of existing programs. In most institutional cases in one study, faculty committees undertook thorough review of new program proposals but in several instances exhibited some tendency to pass on difficult decisions to the campus administration and then to criticize the administration's decision (Barak 1982, p. 15).

Faculty participate in the review of existing programs within their departmental unit when that unit is being reviewed and as members of committees external to the department when programs external to the department are being reviewed. The particulars of structure vary a great deal from campus to campus.

Faculty have generally been hesitant to use criteria other than narrowly academic criteria in the review of existing academic programs, but they must acknowledge some economic criteria in the coming years if they are to exercise significant influence in program review and academic planning. In the climate of the 1980s, faculty should endorse balanced program review conducted by faculty that weighs both academic and financial considerations. Such review would help protect against budgetarily motivated imbalances in program expansions and contractions (Strohm 1983).

Universities have tried a number of structural arrangements to highlight institutionwide planning and to emphasize faculty participation at that level. During the 1970s, West Virginia University provided special visibility by establishing a University Council on Planning that included nine faculty, three students, and three administrators serving ex officio. The university senate recommended two faculty for each seat to the president, and the president chose from that list. Every effort was made to emphasize the expectation that council members would bring a broad perspective to university plans and issues and would serve as representatives of the university rather than as representatives of a particular constituency (Kieft 1978, pp. 27–28).

The literature on planning, which has grown rapidly during the 1970s and 1980s, describes a great variety of approaches to strengthening planning. Two of these approaches seem particularly amenable to faculty participation—formal democratic planning and incentive planning. A formal democratic approach involves a comprehensive planning process that requires all departments to submit their plans to the college and all colleges to submit their plans to the central administration (Heydinger 1980). Such a process depends on the creativity and vision of the faculty of each department and assumes that simultaneous consideration of each unit's plans will result in the emergence of ideas best suited to the institution. The primary appeal of this approach is its openness and consistency with the norms of academic governance, but it remains to be seen whether the approach can live up to expectations regarding effectiveness (Heydinger 1980). The National Center for Higher Education Management Systems has worked extensively on formal democratic approaches, pro-

ducing a handbook on academic and program planning (Kieft, Armijo, and Bucklew 1978) and two studies of the implementation process (Armijo et al. 1980; Kieft 1978).

Incentive planning builds on the belief that departmental units that very directly involve faculty in decision making will be most effective if they are free to design and select their own path to a desired university goal. The central administration must determine overall goals and mission with appropriate input and participation and design incentives responsive to that mission (Heydinger 1980). Incentive planning has had some positive effects where implemented but has not been widely adopted in higher education because of complexities in designing incentives and uncertainties about its impact on the core arts and science disciplines (Heydinger 1980; Zemsky, Porter, and Oedel 1978).

Strategic planning is a recent variant on planning that emphasizes to a greater extent than planning the opportunities and constraints flowing from environmental factors and strong leadership from the chief executive. While recognizing the appropriateness of looking more closely at external factors and emphasizing strong leadership, some analysts of the planning process have expressed concern about whether strategic planning assumes much in the way of faculty participation and influence and about the nature of likely future developments. The literature on strategic planning is relatively new and thus still in the advocacy stage but ultimately will be forced to come to grips with questions on the implications for participation and leadership style of more widespread or longer-term implementation (Miller 1983). Some alteration in the terminology and perspective of strategic planning is necessary to more accurately reflect the characteristics of higher education (Cope 1981). If higher education were to call such planning "open systems planning," for example, it might help foster expectations for widespread and active involvement of faculty and other campus constituencies and help delicately adjust the underlying ideas (pp. 55–56). Others believe, however, that faculty are unlikely to have much impact on strategic planning (Baldridge and Okimi 1982).

More definitive judgments about the adequacy of the answers that the strategic planning literature and practice provide to questions of faculty participation and influence must be reserved at this time. That literature does include some elements of faculty participation (see, for example, Caruthers and Lott 1981, pp. 47–63; and Keller 1983, pp. 61–62). What Keller terms "Joint Big Decision Committees" have been formed on some campuses as a way to involve faculty in important strategic decisions; their work and membership are widely known, but deliberations are kept secret.

Whether Joint Big Decision Committees can provide for significant faculty participation in strategic planning is questionable. Given their smallness and the privacy of their deliberations, such committees would exclude too many potential participants who have special expertise or are significantly affected by a decision; they might also contribute to the atrophy of the academic senate (Powers and Powers 1984). Overall, Joint Big Decision Committees could hinder rather than help the development of a decision-making culture that provides for the broad involvement of faculty. The question then becomes, "How can necessary strategic planning be undertaken in participatory fashion without creating permanent, exclusionary structures that may become counterproductive?" (Powers and Powers 1984, p. 50). One suggestion is to institutionalize the institution's planning process and to promote a participatory culture, replacing a single permanent committee with a broad range of responsibilities with a series of temporary or sometimes permanent committees with more narrowly defined charges operating in the overall framework provided by an umbrella committee. Committee deliberations should be open and committee membership more fluid (Powers and Powers 1984).

Budgeting
At most institutions, faculty do not participate much in or have significant influence upon institutionwide budgetary processes (Austin and Gamson 1983, p. 32; M. E. Brown in "Four Issues" 1982, pp. 7A–8A; Lee 1978, p. 42). This low level of participation has some relationship to administrative resistance, but it can also be tied to deep faculty ambivalence about participating in decisions for which they may be blamed and about participating with students in

decisions where the economic interests of faculty and students may be strongly in conflict (Millett 1978, pp. 207–8, 227).

Both faculty and new academic affairs administrators are handicapped in participating in the budgetary process by their lack of knowledge of that process. A cooperative effort between the American Association of University Professors and the National Association of College and University Budget Officers has resulted in a primer for those new to the budgetary process. The primer (Meisinger and Dubeck 1984) provides background on substantive issues, process dynamics, and technical tools, emphasizing that questions of how faculty members can influence the budgetary process involve a number of interrelated factors. The authors recognize that knowledge of the climate in which events occur, the sequence of events, and budgetary actors is a necessary but not sufficient condition to influence the process. Over time, participants become more skilled in and sophisticated about how to phrase and raise questions so as to maximize their impact. As it frequently takes two to three years for an individual to be sufficiently knowledgeable to make a major contribution and have a significant impact, frequent turnover on campuswide budgetary committees tends to significantly reduce the opportunity for effective faculty participation and influence (Meisinger and Dubeck 1984, chap. 4).

Three broad categories encompass most of the questions asked by participants in budgeting: expenditure plans, sources of revenue, and hidden costs. As priorities affecting programs and activities are the heart of the budget, a number of useful questions might be asked about such priorities. Questions focus on variations in workload and technology, the methodology for determining faculty and staff salary adjustments, the effect on programmatic quality of using part-time and temporary faculty, and alternate ways of administering sabbaticals (Meisinger and Dubeck 1984, chap. 4).

University budgets have some flexibility, and they encourage the use of certain strategies to meet a fiscal crisis. Sources of flexibility include creating a central pool of resources, using temporary or part-time faculty, and engaging in sponsored research and training (Meisinger and Dubeck 1984, chap. 5). Strategies for meeting a fiscal crisis are grouped into three categories reflecting the time available to achieve the reduction, the range of options available within that time, and the specific characteristics of the institution. The first category covers the short term of one to three years and emphasizes cash management. The second relates to an intermediate term, two to six years, and focuses on personnel management. The third deals with the long term, three to nine years, and focuses on program priorities, including a significant reallocation of resources (Meisinger and Dubeck 1984, chap. 6).

Faculty believe that significant barriers to faculty influence on the budgetary process arise out of the increasing centralization of that process in the offices of the president and academic vice president. The problem of faculty access could perhaps be solved without reducing the centralization of budgetary decision making through the use of Keller's Joint Big Decision Committee. Such a committee would advise the president on major decisions requiring the integration of planning and budgetary factors; it would be a new kind of cabinet government that could provide a way for quick and vigorous presidential action with faculty advice and guidance. For such a committee to work well, however, faculty will need to recognize the need for executive authority for overall planning and priorities and to commit themselves fully to the principle of confidentiality. Further, administrators must give the faculty who serve on the committee an opportunity to apply their full critical and analytical expertise to the issues at hand (Keller 1983).

Retrenchment and Financial Exigency
A sizable literature on retrenchment and financial exigency that describes institutional experience and analyzes applicable legal principles has developed in the past 10 years. Although definitions of financial exigency in that literature vary somewhat, they all refer to a set of institutional financial circumstances of such gravity that the layoff or termination of tenured or tenure-track faculty is necessary.

Most of that literature emphasizes the importance of administrative communication and consultation with faculty. University administrations greatly increase the acceptability of retrenchment and minimize declines in faculty morale if they consult with and heed the advice of faculty while designing measures of retrenchment (Hammond and Tompkins 1983; Williams, Olswang, and Hargett *In press*). Boards of trustees benefit from developing procedures to be used in case of financial exigency before those conditions actually arise, and the procedures should be developed in consultation with faculty and provide for consultation with faculty when conditions requiring retrenchment actually arise (Groves 1977).

Not surprisingly, faculty are ambivalent about participating in planning for retrenchment or financial exigency; faculty at some universities have chosen to participate while faculty at other universities have not. Faculty reluctance to participate is more likely on unionized campuses, where the bargaining agent may discourage participation (Pondrom 1981). Faculty who have participated in the development of a policy for retrenchment and financial exigency emphasize the need for each institution to tailor a policy to its own missions, history, and programmatic needs. The faculty must struggle with the internal dynamics of their own campus and must develop their own support networks of individuals and groups (Moore 1978).

Issues about the elimination of programs become particularly contentious during a period of retrenchment or financial exigency. Institutions benefit from having a formal statement that defines the steps of a program review process and who has final authority to initiate the termination. The process must specify who should be consulted and on precisely what issues during the process of program termination. Carrying out the process exactly as it is written is the best defense that administrators have to attacks on review and evaluation procedures (Powers and Powers 1983, pp. 83–97).

Consultation with faculty committees is most effective when faculty are asked about methods and criteria to be used rather than about specific programs or people to be terminated (Mortimer, Bagshaw, and Masland 1985). Although faculty will sometimes participate in the identification of programs to be closed after an extensive debate about decisional process and implementation, they will absolutely refuse to participate in identification of specific colleagues to be terminated (Mortimer, Bagshaw, and Masland 1985).

The courts have held that faculty members do not have a constitutional right to participate in the determination of whether a financial exigency exists or in the implementation of resultant cutbacks. The burden of proof is on institutions to demonstrate that a bona fide financial exigency exists and that faculty members were selected for termination on a basis that was neither arbitrary nor capricious. Courts have usually found institutional actions acceptable if they are consistent with well-developed written policies, whether or not those policies make any provision for faculty participation. Although faculty participation can facilitate a finding of good faith, a higher education institution is not legally compelled to directly involve faculty unless such involvement is specified in institutional policies, contracts, or negotiations (Johnson 1981; Van Gieson and Zirkel 1981).

Institutions are bound by the AAUP Recommended Institutional Regulation on financial exigency only if they explicitly adopt that regulation as their own. The desirability of adopting that regulation has long been debated (Furniss 1977; Mortimer and Tierney 1979, pp. 41–43; White 1983).

Concluding Analysis

Curriculum and faculty personnel status are the two areas of institutional decision making in which faculty have had and continue to have the broadest role and the greatest influence. Protecting the strong faculty participatory role in this area is likely to require, however, a more concerted effort by faculty and administrators working together to address issues of general education, staffing quality and flexibility, and some aspects of faculty conduct. The resolution of these issues is central to faculty credibility and institutional viability.

Within the past 15 years, faculty participation in the selection and evaluation of administrators and in planning has become relatively well established. Faculty participation is a significant element in the process by which presidents are selected and a normative factor against which candidates are evaluated. Faculty ambivalence about integrating financial with academic factors, which has tended to restrict faculty participation and influence in some stages of planning and program review, is also beginning to recede. The healthy debate about the best mechanisms and approaches for providing for faculty participation in strategic planning suggests good prospects for balance between executive leadership and broad participation in the approaches to strategic planning developing on many campuses.

Although faculty have been frustrated by what they perceive to be lack of involvement or ineffective participation in processes of budgeting and of planning for retrenchment, some groundwork has been laid for greater and more effective faculty participation. Faculty have begun to take steps in concert with administrators to gain a better understanding of the technical bases and dynamics of the budgetary process, thus reducing a previous major handicap. Boards of trustees and university administrators are also becoming more sophisticated about the importance of process considerations in handling retrenchment and the greater acceptability of retrenchment if faculty are consulted when general procedures are developed and when implementation becomes necessary.

Although most of the literature about faculty participation in decision making focuses on campus-level decision making, more attention is now being given to faculty participation in decision making at the system level in multicampus systems and at the level of statewide coordinating boards (Floyd 1982, pp. 8–9). Interest in issues about participation at those levels has somewhat paralleled the growth in awareness of how decisions made at those levels affect campuses and their faculties.

Approximately 70 percent of U.S. public senior college and university campuses are a part of multicampus systems overseen by a single governing board (Berdahl and Gove 1982, p. 21). Some states have a single statewide multicampus state university system, while others have two or more multicampus state systems. States without a single statewide governing board frequently have a statewide coordinating board that performs selected functions related to program approval, budget recommendation, and master planning for the public senior institutions as a whole and sometimes also has some limited functions related to private higher education.

Concern about faculty participation in decision making at these levels has been present as a relatively minor theme in some of the earlier reports on the sharing of authority in higher education; it has only more recently received concentrated attention. Formal faculty participation at this level can take three forms: (1) direct membership (voting or nonvoting) on the board itself; (2) a formal systemwide senate or statewide committee; or (3) extensive faculty participation in ad hoc and standing technical working committees (Berdahl and Gove 1982).

The alternative of a formal systemwide senate or statewide committee has been of strongest interest in theory and in practice. This preference is reflected in the statement on the faculty role on state-level boards approved by the council of the American Association of University Professors, which recommends that faculty participation be provided through a systemwide senate (in the case of governing boards) and a faculty advisory committee (in the case of coordinating boards) (AAUP 1984).

System Level
Although campus senates typically have a few legislative

The alternative of a formal systemwide senate or statewide committee has been of strongest interest in theory and in practice.

functions in addition to advisory functions, a systemwide senate serves almost exclusively advisory functions. It typically provides advice to the system chief executive and to the system board (Lee and Bowen 1971, p. 194).

The systemwide senate is far from universal in college and university systems. Only seven of the 20 states that have a single statewide governing board have provided for a systemwide senate or its equivalent (Berdahl and Gove 1982, p. 21). Systemwide senates are most common in segmental systems that include the primary state research campus but do not cover the whole state.

Perhaps the most difficult question multicampus systems face in establishing a systemwide senate is whether representation is to be based on the number of faculty or on the equality of the campuses. Frequently a compromise is reached: Representation is related in some way to the number of faculty but smaller campuses are also given some compensatory weight (Lee and Bowen 1971, pp. 186–90).

Faculty are quite ambivalent toward systemwide senates, and that ambivalence arises out of the higher priority faculty attach to the campus senate (Lee and Bowen 1971). Although campus faculties are appropriately protective of local prerogatives, they need also to recognize the legitimacy and importance of faculty participation systemwide (pp. 449–50).

Faculty senate leaders continue to seek ways to link the senates of various state institutions in states where each institution has its own governing board or where two or more multicampus systems are found. A confederation of campus senates in Ohio, for example, contributed to an understanding of comparative structures and methods of faculty governance, helped address sensitive issues like faculty codes of ethics or conduct that local senates were hesitant to initiate, and provided information about developments on the state level to local senates (Moore 1975).

State Level
Three of the 28 states with statewide coordinating boards have established faculty advisory committees. In Illinois and Maryland, the faculty advisory committee includes members from the private sector; in Connecticut, membership does not include the private sector (Berdahl and Gove 1982). Faculty advisory committees become involved in

state coordinating board policy through reaction to position papers prepared by board staff, initiation of in-depth studies by the board staff, and initiation of its own studies (Mumper 1983).

Faculty advisory committees perform several roles: communication, advocacy, and policy. They communicate campus views to the coordinating board staff and relay information on activities by state agencies to campus faculty. They can be influential in the role of advocate so long as they speak on broad issues of educational quality, but as soon as they speak to the narrower employment interests of faculty, they cut themselves out of the process (Mumper 1983). None of the faculty advisory committees have developed a continuing influence on policy development in their states because of the short time frame in which most decisions are made and the complexity of the environment in which the committee must operate. When strong conflicts between the state and faculty perspectives occur, the committee must attempt to reduce and mediate the conflict between its two constituencies (pp. 300–301).

What are the determinants of the faculty advisory committee's influence and the constraints upon that influence? Legitimacy is related to the ability of the committee to achieve access to and professional relationships with staff of the state coordinating board. The legitimacy of some members is weakened by their selection by institutional administrators rather than by the constituent group; credibility is increased by an established and respected election system. Members of faculty advisory committees face the paradox that to influence policy they must maintain access but also maintain some distance from the staff of the state coordinating board. Committee members must therefore make special efforts to avoid the appearance of cooptation (Mumper 1983). Constraints on the faculty advisory committee's ability to perform its various roles include the suspicion existing between faculty, institutions, and state coordinating boards, and the unwillingness of many faculty to participate in its activities (Mumper 1983).

Balancing faculty involvement and state needs is particularly difficult when a state must plan for retrenchment. State political leaders seek what they regard as independent leadership from the state coordinating board; broad participation may therefore be a formula for political rejection of the resulting plan. On the other hand, if the plan does not reflect some faculty and administrative aspirations but limits itself to identifying areas for cutback or elimination, faculty members have little or no reason to support it (Folger 1980, p. 60). It therefore remains to be seen whether statewide coordinating boards will involve faculty advisory committees to any significant degree in any planning they do for retrenchment.

The experience with faculty advisory committees to statewide coordinating boards is too limited and too short for conclusions to be drawn about their effectiveness as a mechanism for faculty participation in policy making of statewide coordinating boards. ''No one should expect spectacular early results—it may take several years before outcomes justify the additional procedural complexities'' (Berdahl and Gove 1982, p. 24).

PARTICIPATION AND CENTRALIZATION/DECENTRALIZATION

This chapter examines the relationship between faculty participation in institutional decision making and the centralization or decentralization of decision making. The first section notes centralizing factors, includes a rationale for minimizing centralization, and examines issues of managerial philosophy. The second section notes positive factors about the decentralization of decision making and some significant limiting factors upon decentralization.

Centralization

Faculty, administrators, and many other higher education personnel are concerned that decision making in higher education institutions has in some ways become more centralized in the 1970s and 1980s in response to a combination of internal and external pressures. Elements in this centralization include campuswide academic senates, a new managerial orientation, the presence of collective bargaining agents for faculty in some institutions, and increasing powers for system-level and state-level higher education authorities.

Many faculty are uncomfortable with the centralization of faculty power away from the department/college level to the campuswide level (Millett 1978). Even in a decision area like curriculum where faculty exercise the primary influence, the issue of the level at which faculty will make the decision—department, college, or campus—is often strongly contested (Mortimer and McConnell 1978, p. 128).

A shift in locus of decision making from lower to higher levels of the institution reduces the visibility of both faculty participation and the decision-making process itself. The faculty's sense of access is reduced when most faculty participation is achieved through representatives and committees rather than through direct input. Faculty ties to the process and a sense of participation become more distant and abstract (Dykes 1968, p. 14).

Many commentators on organizational centralization/decentralization believe that organizational centralization has become a major problem for the operations and adaptability of modern organizations because a highly centralized organization does not fully engage the talents or cooperative instincts of employees (Kanter 1983; Naisbitt 1982; Peters and Waterman 1982). This perspective on centralization has not been applied in detail to higher education institutions (Austin and Gamson 1983, pp. 68–70).

The administrative instinct to further centralize institutional decision making varies across institutions and over time, tending to peak at times of major institutional crisis. Faculty believe that they must be especially vigilant on issues of centralization during a period of crisis and strongly resist such initiatives (Baldridge 1982). More generally, some faculty suggest efforts to closely question the specifics of managerial philosophy articulated at any particular institution in an effort to discourage the development of a viewpoint that heavily emphasizes centralized decision making. When the desirability of strong executive initiative is stressed, faculty following such an approach would ask very specific questions as to how it is going to be done, what provision will be made for the participation of faculty and other campus constituencies, and the specific effect any new educational initiatives might have on educational policy. Although faculty recognize the importance of strong action-oriented leadership at the top, they also wish to make clear the desirability of broad participation and the need to develop shared goals (Miller 1983).

Decentralization

Although further centralization of decision making should be avoided, a general decentralization of decision making is probably neither desirable nor feasible in higher education institutions. The literature on decentralization of decision making identifies a number of features of higher education organization that make decentralization desirable and other factors that limit its usefulness—all of which implies that decisions need be made case by case on whether or not decentralization of decision making is appropriate in any particular instance.

Strong arguments have been presented for the generally positive effects of decentralization on organizational climate (Foote, Mayer, and associates 1968, chap. 5) and as a positive management style (Richman and Farmer 1974, p. 247). Decentralization of decision making to departmental units is regarded as a particularly desirable way to recognize the importance of faculty participation, increases in morale that come from a feeling of ownership of the decision, strong faculty preferences for department-level decision making, and students' preferences for decisions to be made at a level of organization where they believe they have good access (Baldridge and Tierney 1979, p. 160).

Some specific organizational characteristics limit the institutional usefulness of decentralizing much decision making to the departmental level: departmental provincialism that does not take into consideration the needs of the broader institution, the lack of institutional orientation by department chairs, and the lack of an effective institutional reward system for department chairs (Baldridge and Tierney 1979, p. 160).

Too much decision making by institutional segments like departments can make it difficult to achieve a sense of institutional coherence (Epstein 1974). Segmented decision making can aggravate the natural split among disciplines, making it hard to protect general education and to foster cooperation between disciplines. An institution concerned about aggravating such a split does not completely decentralize matters of balance of academic programs and educational offerings to academic departments, as groups of constituents external to the department have legitimate interests in such matters (Mortimer and McConnell 1978, p. 255). If certain academic decisions are decentralized to designated academic units, it is desirable that the extent to which the decisions of the departmental unit conform to the institution's educational priorities be reviewed at least periodically (McConnell and Mortimer 1971, p. 169). Unfortunately, the short-term temptations to decentralize are strong in higher education (as in many other organizational settings) because decentralization leads to a short-term reduction in conflict, with any problems posed for the overall health of the institution coming much farther down the road (Pfeffer 1978).

Concluding Analysis
The decentralization of substantial decision-making authority to the departmental level that has occurred in the last 25 years has tended to provide opportunities for faculty participation at the departmental level that are especially satisfying and promote effective departmental functioning. At the same time, the reality is that institutional coherence requires that institutionwide decision making be more than a simple aggregation of the decisions of departments and

other institutional subunits. (Institutionwide concerns about maintaining the coherence of the undergraduate curriculum reflecting that determination are further addressed in a subsequent chapter.)

Given needs for institutional coherence, any further decentralization of decision making in higher education institutions must necessarily be very selective in spite of temptations to reduce conflict in the short term through such decentralization.

A sizable literature focuses on joint participation of administrators and professional employees in institutional decision-making. In that literature, the proper role of organizational leadership is increasingly seen as managing the decision-making process within the organization rather than as direct decision making. This perspective suggests a process view of decision making and an orientation toward relatively broad participation while not suggesting organizational leaders have given up their hierarchical powers, and it is expressed both within the organizational theory literature, which draws mainly upon the business experience (Thompson and Tuden 1974; Wynn and Guditus 1984), and within higher education literature (Mortimer and McConnell 1978, p. 275; Powers and Powers 1983).

Most of the higher education literature reviewed here assumes the appropriateness of joint participation. Within this context, higher education leaders see themselves as managers of the institutional decision process and focus their energies on four crucial decision elements—rebuilding collegial foundations, shaping the consultative framework, increasing the availability of information, and facilitating group deliberations.

Rebuilding Collegial Foundations

Articulation of a set of shared values and goals is perhaps the most important administrative leadership function in a higher education institution (as well as in any other organization) (Burns 1978; Cyert 1980; Kanter 1983; McConnell and Mortimer 1971; Mortimer and McConnell 1978; Peters and Waterman 1982; Vroom 1983), and the higher education literature of the middle 1980s strongly urges that a firmer base be provided for collegial decision making in higher education institutions than has been perceived to exist in recent years. Collegial decision making requires consensus on fundamental premises, participants who deal with each other face to face with great mutual respect, and the time and opportunity for discussion. Strengthening the collegial base suggests reducing the extent of organizational specialization that has existed in recent years and reaffirming certain basic academic values.

The most frequently mentioned factor in the decline of collegiality is the increased specialization and departmental orientation of faculty since World War II (Austin and Gamson 1983). As faculty became more oriented toward their own discipline and organizational unit and less oriented toward the institution's overall purposes, the undergraduate curriculum became more specialized and less attention was paid to general education. Faculty interacted primarily with departmental colleagues, had little regular contact outside the department, and no longer shared many fundamental premises with faculty in other departments (Austin and Gamson 1983). Other factors reducing collegiality are changes in the academic labor market that work against the tradition of long-term employment, the increased bureaucratization of higher education institutions, and the development of separate administrative career paths (Wyer 1982).

During 1984 and 1985, the reports of national study commissions placed heavy emphasis on and gave additional impetus to broadening the undergraduate curriculum, especially its general education core, to restore a sense of purpose to the undergraduate curriculum and to the institution as a whole (Kerr 1984; Project on Redefining 1985; Study Group 1984). The efforts of faculty and administrators to design and implement stronger curricula will help build faculty and administrative ties across the dividing lines between disciplines, which in turn will help build mutual respect and consensus on fundamental principles.

The Association of American Colleges project report on the baccalaureate degree (Project on Redefining 1985) criticizes academic leaders for having acquiesced in recent years to the focusing of faculty attention upon the departmental level and for thus neglecting to turn faculty toward a sense of commitment about their larger responsibilities to their institutions. It calls for institutional administrators to seize the initiative by appointing faculty task forces to study general education requirements with the clear expectation that significant recommendations will result and will be implemented. It also emphasizes the collective responsibility of all campus constituencies for curriculum reform:

Faculties, administrators, and trustees have a collective responsibility to their institutions and their students. It is a corporate responsibility that can be carried out effectively and imaginatively only if each group recognizes that, in the end, its role is to educate students who for a

*time pass under their joint nurture. The board must over-
see. The presidents and their assistants must lead. The
faculty must face and live with the substantive issues. In
the end, however, the performance of the faculty will
decide whether the integrity of the curriculum will be
restored* (Project on Redefining 1985, p. 18).

The primary reservation faculty have about recent cri-
tiques of curriculum is that they tend to isolate curriculum
and instruction from other higher education problems aris-
ing inside and outside the institution (Benjamin 1985, p.
28). In particular, it has been suggested that more needs to
be made of problems of the liberal arts professoriate, such
as low morale and a deteriorating work environment, that
greatly complicate efforts to revitalize the liberal arts core
of the curriculum (Schuster and Bowen 1985, pp. 19–20).

Some higher education analysts have called attention to
Japanese management styles currently receiving much
attention in the popular business management literature as
a way to focus attention on an administrative style consistent with collegial decision making within American higher
education institutions (Chait 1982a; Powers and Powers
1983, pp. 42–45; Wyer 1982). These analysts cite William
Ouchi's *Theory Z* (1981) as the seminal work on Japanese
management methods applied to American business and
industry. Ouchi emphasizes a decision-making process that
typically involves broad participation and is oriented
toward reaching consensus. The holistic orientation con-
tributes to employees' dealing with each other as whole
human beings, thus contributing to an egalitarian atmosphere. Although Theory Z organizations do use hierarchical methods of control, the emphasis is on the replacing of
hierarchical direction by self-direction to a significant
extent. This orientation enhances commitment, loyalty,
and motivation (Ouchi 1981). Guides to the application of
Theory Z in higher education summarize the main points of
Ouchi's work and spell out specific actions needed to
implement Theory Z (Holt and Wagner 1983; Redinbaugh
and Redinbaugh 1983; Spiro and Campbell 1983).

The implementation of Theory Z in higher education provides opportunities and obstacles. The application of Theory Z will have little effect so long as faculty continue to
operate through departments as though they were craft

*Ouchi
emphasizes a
decision-
making
process that
typically
involves broad
participation
and is
oriented
toward
reaching
consensus.*

union members and so long as university administrators remain generally uninterested in and ignorant of techniques for designing participatory decision processes (Nichols 1982a, 1982b). In general, major research universities have historically stayed closest to the collegial model and can be expected to make the greatest efforts to move closer toward that model (Chait 1982b).

Although Theory Z and other Japanese management approaches may have some utility in drawing attention to issues about the relationship between administrative style and collegiality, they also have negative implications that may limit their symbolic utility. Although, for example, Japanese management style has some salutary effects in building commitment to an organization, it also is a possible threat to historic American concepts of individual freedom (Staw 1983). In practice, much of the consultation in Japanese-style management occurs after a decision has been made and therefore serves primarily to achieve broader ratification of managers' decisions and to provide for early communication of that decision within the organization (Pucik and Hatvany 1983).

Shaping the Consultative Framework
The higher education literature of the past 10 years reflects a growing consensus about necessary characteristics of the consultative process and, in general terms, the steps to be taken in that process. A set of understandings is evolving about where very broad consultation is useful and where consultation is appropriately limited. Special attention has also been given to provisions for consultation in crises and for handling the conflict that often surfaces during consultation.

Six criteria must be met if adequate consultative opportunities are to be provided to faculty:

1. Consultation should occur early in the decision-making process.
2. Faculty and administrators should jointly formulate procedures for consultation.
3. Faculty must have time to consider and formulate responses to the issues posed.
4. All relevant information with the exception of items concerning the peer review of personnel must be made available.

5. Adequate feedback must be provided to the consulting group when recommendations are not acceptable or when no action is being taken.
6. The final decision must be communicated to all interested campus constituencies (Mortimer and McConnell 1978, pp. 275–80).

Faculty are particularly frustrated by considerations of timing. Sometimes they perceive that they are consulted only after a course of action has been decided upon or that too many committees are formed just before the summer break to deal with long-standing issues (Mortimer and McConnell 1978).

Eight distinctive steps can be identified in the consultative process—identification of the problem, definition of the problem, analysis of alternatives, drafting of a position paper, circulation of a position paper, referral of the position paper to internal governance bodies, deliberation of the governance bodies, and final approval by the institutional president (Powers and Powers 1983, pp. 9–16).

Faculty and administrators must agree on guidelines about issues that do and do not require consultation. For those issues requiring consultation, it must also be determined how broad that consultation should be. Matters involving formulation of policy that will affect large numbers of individuals require broad consultation (Powers and Powers 1983, chap. 4). Participation in decision making should also be broad when views on the issues are conflicting, when relevant information is dispersed widely within the organization, when strong institutional norms for participation are involved, and when personal commitment is necessary for implementation of the decision (Chaffee 1981). Efforts should be made to include those who will be affected by the decision, those who will implement the decision, those who are experts on the issue on which the decision is to be made, and campus opinion leaders (Chaffee 1981).

The higher education literature reflects a growing consensus that participation is appropriately limited under a number of circumstances. Participation probably will not even be sought when accepted routines or traditional solutions are acceptable in the academic culture or when decisions are highly technical and do not affect faculty (Chaffee

1981; Powers and Powers 1983, chap. 4). Participation is also appropriately limited if the decision maker does not intend to pay close attention to the advice given, as faculty regard solicitation of advice under those circumstances as manipulative (Chaffee 1983).

Although broad participation is reasonably restricted in an urgent situation (Chaffee 1981, p. 14), consensus has not been reached about what constitutes sufficient urgency to appropriately limit participation. Faculty have pushed and will continue to push for an extremely narrow construction of "urgent" and will be leery of the classification of any matter as urgent. Most decision making in a crisis involves one or more of the following conditions: time constraints, an emotional component, public attention, or involvement from outside the university (Powers and Powers 1983, chap. 7). In such circumstances, every attempt should be made to come as close as possible to maintaining accepted processes and procedures (Powers and Powers 1983). Generally, ad hoc processes will not be regarded as legitimate and may be difficult to defend in court if an aggrieved party sues. Although some of the consultation may need to be more private than under ordinary circumstances, campus constituencies must be informed that consultation is underway and that progress reports will be issued. Administrators should be quite active in those discussions so that those consulted understand fully the importance of responding to the institution's broader needs and so that they can actively negotiate solutions when reaching a solution is difficult. In a crisis, the long-term rather than short-term effects of policies considered must be examined. Further, a postcrisis inventory should be taken to assess the operation of the decision-making process during the crisis to ensure that good communication and coordination were maintained and to deal with any relationships that may have been damaged during the crisis (Powers and Powers 1983, chap. 7).

Automatic rejection of wide participation in instances where such a pattern would bring conflict out into the open is not advised. Bringing conflict into the open can help clarify issues, generate innovative solutions, and promote commitment to the decision and to the institution (Chaffee 1981).

Increasing the Availability of Information

Faculty seek to increase the amount of information they provide to decision makers and to be provided a better informational base on which to formulate the advice they provide administrators. In the case of the former, they wish administrators to better understand their preferences on process and policy. In the latter, they seek a more diverse informational base on their own institution and more information about the experiences of faculty at other institutions in solving problems.

In one case, procedures were developed to provide an informational flow from the faculty of a university business college to decision makers in the form of opinions or preferences about the role of the business dean (Pollay, Taylor, and Thompson 1976). The methodology used to investigate the issue involved two stages. First, small group discussions were held to identify issues crucial to the administration of the school. Second, a questionnaire was developed, administered, and interpreted to systematically assess the preferences of faculty as to how the dean's role should be constructed (Pollay, Taylor, and Thompson 1976).

Faculty frequently seek greater informational support for institutional committee service and especially more information about students' interests and budgets in an easily understandable format (Andrew 1979). Some institutions have made special attempts to undertake systematic information sharing. An annual "fact book" is one useful way of sharing information broadly on campus. Such a volume presents a broad spectrum of descriptive information about institutional characteristics, such as mission, organizational structure, students, faculty, academic programs, fiscal resources, and physical facilities (Smith 1980).

It has been suggested that greater administrative attention be focused on the effective and efficient provision of relevant data to academic senates and other collegially oriented decision groups. Issues about priorities for the collection of information continue to arise because campus institutional research offices are usually understaffed and are hard pressed to provide regular reports to the institution's central administration (Spitzberg 1980, p. 15).

Faculty also continue to seek mechanisms to help increase their familiarity with the range of national practice as one reference point in identifying alternate solutions to problems and their relative advantages and disadvantages (Soles 1973). The American Association of University Professors developed a "faculty in governance support system" in 1981 to provide such a resource base on national practice. It was designed to include information gathering, research, communication, and some aspects of networking. It would also collect data on actual practices, develop alternative models, gather information on substantive issues that arose on campuses, do nonduplicative research, sponsor closely focused seminars, develop faculty governance internships modeled after American Council on Education administrative internships, and publish a newsletter to foster cooperation and networking ("The Future" 1982).

The AAUP, however, was not successful in assembling sufficient funds from foundations or institutional sources to allow implementation of the system. The undertaking faced several obstacles: the wide range of institutions to be served, a shortage of institutional funds for membership, and the possible reluctance of some campuses to enter into a formal relationship with the AAUP ("Faculty Governance" 1981). The AAUP currently informally performs some of the resource center functions through its committee on university government.

Facilitating Group Deliberations

An increased consultative and consensual orientation to the decision process suggests the importance of administrators' holding frequent meetings to discuss issues with faculty and using approaches emphasizing group problem solving. Meetings are viewed as the best mechanism for sharing information, engaging in joint problem solving, and coordinating action (Pascale and Athos 1981, pp. 130–31; Wynn and Guditus 1984, p. 211).

A sizable organizational theory literature provides insights into various aspects of group decision making, including factors affecting problem-solving capacity, task-oriented leadership functions, group maintenance functions, patterns of sharing group leadership, obstacles to rational evaluation of decision alternatives, and suggestions for improving group decision making (Bradford 1976; Kanter 1983, pp. 256–71; Wynn and Guditus 1984; Yukl 1981, chap. 9; Zander 1977, 1982).

A number of task-oriented leadership functions and group maintenance functions must be performed to focus and guide the group's activities. The task-oriented leadership functions include initiating various activities, stimulating communication within the group, clarifying and summarizing points made in group discussion, and taking the consensus of the group. The group maintenance functions include gatekeeping, harmonizing, providing support, setting standards for the group, and analyzing the process of group interaction (Yukl 1981, pp. 239–44).

Organizational theorists differ on the emphasis to be placed on group maintenance and task-oriented functions and on the feasibility of group members' sharing the leadership (Yukl 1981, pp. 244–48). Group-centered leadership is appealing but requires considerable skill and maturity on the part of the administrative leader and the group members to work well (p. 266).

Successful leaders take a number of steps to provide guidance in group problem solving: presenting a problem in goal-oriented terms, presenting a problem free of any implied decision, encouraging participation of all group members, creating a free enough atmosphere for disagreement and conflict on ideals and proposals to be expressed, and taking periodic action to keep the group on the problem, thus giving the group a sense of accomplishment (Maier 1963, p. 163; Yukl 1981, pp. 248–53).

Groups encounter four typical kinds of obstacles during the evaluation of and choice among decision alternatives: hasty decisions, incomplete participation, polarization, and superficial action planning (Yukl 1981, pp. 257–65). Problems of incomplete participation and polarization are formidable in a number of organizations, and higher education is no exception. Some group members may not present information that is pertinent to a decision if they are afraid of openly opposing a vocal minority, especially if the group leader or another person with high status openly supports the apparently dominant position. This situation can result in a false consensus and little acceptance of the decision. The leader can facilitate more complete participation by encouraging each group member to participate in the discussion and by discouraging social pressure tactics. The leader can also encourage the group to attempt to reach a consensus rather than deciding on the basis of a simple majority (Yukl 1981, pp. 259–61). Polarization occurs when a group divides itself into two opposing factions, each committed to its own preferred alternative. Discussion tends to focus primarily on the differences between the positions of the two factions. Polarization can result in one of two very undesirable outcomes—prolonged stalemate or a decision forced by the politically stronger faction.

The leader's capacity to deal with polarization depends on his or her alertness to early signs and early action to reduce tension and hostility. The leader concentrates on harmonizing behavior by pointing out areas of agreement, discouraging derogatory comments, and restating comments that may have been misunderstood. The leader can point out to the group that it seems to be heading toward polarization and ask for discussion about ways to avoid it. The organization theory literature also identifies two specific procedures to prevent polarization and to avoid a stalemate when the group is having difficulty reaching agreement about rival alternatives—posting advantages and solution integration. The first procedure requires each member to consider the positive aspects of both alternatives identified, thus delaying criticism. It helps to depersonalize the discussion and allows the group to develop a deeper understanding of both alternatives. The second procedure encourages the group to develop an integrative solution that reflects the principal features, if not the entirety, of the previous alternatives. The specific variety of the second procedure used depends on whether the factions have different objectives and priorities or whether they disagree only about the likely outcomes of the various alternatives (Yukl 1981, pp. 262–64).

Concluding Analysis
Rebuilding collegial foundations poses the greatest challenges for joint faculty and administrative efforts within the next few years, as the bonds of shared values have greatly atrophied in the past 25 years concurrent with the weakening of the undergraduate curriculum and the increasing specialization and departmentalization of faculty. Reports of national study commissions issued in 1984 and 1985 have provided a major boost to articulation of shared goals and values and the implementation of a stronger undergraduate curriculum necessary to rebuilding the collegial founda-

tions for campus decision making. The higher education literature of the late 1980s will reflect the successes and failures of initiatives taken by administrators and faculty to implement the recommendations of those reports.

Most of the literature on rebuilding collegial foundations, shaping the consultative framework, and increasing the availability of information is specific to higher education and highly normative. With the passage of time, reports of experience in implementing the suggestions contained in the literature will enable testing of the norms. Most of the literature on facilitating group deliberations has been formulated without a higher education reference point but has been subject to greater empirical testing in other settings. With the passage of time, the higher education literature should include tests of the extent to which these generalizations are applicable to higher education.

Patterns of faculty interest in participation and willingness to participate are very complex. The extent of faculty interest in participation is not fully known, and faculty have sometimes declined to participate when afforded the opportunity (Austin and Gamson 1983, p. 34; Clark 1968; Dykes 1968; Marshall 1976; Touraine 1974). Faculty members emphasize the importance of extensive faculty participation for the health of the institution but indicate that participation in institutional decision making is a relatively low priority for the use of their own time and the time of their colleagues (Dykes 1968). Generally, faculty members are unaware of actual faculty participation in a number of institutional decision-making activities and are therefore unaware of the actual extent of faculty participation (Dykes 1968).

Faculty frequently express an obligation and the competence to participate but put low priority on actual participation.

The patterns of participation in university senates are similar to those in the American political system more generally. Most of the population is apathetic, but a significant number are interested spectators and a very few are activists. Faculty frequently express an obligation and the competence to participate but put low priority on actual participation (McConnell 1971; McConnell and Mortimer 1971, p. 21). A national survey on the frequency and intensity of faculty participation found that 54 percent of the faculty indicated they were not heavily involved in institutional decision making but 18 percent frequently participated (Baldridge et al. 1978, pp. 75–76). An additional survey of those who identified themselves as frequently participating showed that the higher the academic rank of the faculty member, the greater the amount of formal participation.

Recent years give evidence of fewer perceived opportunities to participate in planning and governance in some types of institutions (Anderson 1983) but also less willingness of faculty to participate in selected governance activities like senates than in the past (Wilson 1979, p. 113).

Although all the sources of faculty ambivalence about participating in institutional decision making are not clear, the literature provides a number of reports about intrinsic satisfactions of and institutional rewards for participation.

Intrinsic Satisfactions
To draw intrinsic satisfaction from participating in decision making, a number of conditions must be met. A faculty

member must understand both the process used to reach a decision and the subject matter about which the decision is being made. The individual must also sense that the decision really is being influenced by the group of which he or she is a part and that the decision is not totally trivial.

The actual circumstances under which faculty participate in institutional decision making are not such that these conditions are consistently met. Cynicism is becoming an increasing problem in higher education institutions because the substance and process of decision making are not sufficiently clear to the direct participants and are not at all evident to most of the faculty on campus (Chaffee 1983, p. 51). A faculty budgetary affairs committee, for example, may feel that it is limited to low-risk and insignificant subjects and excluded from the more fundamental and sensitive subjects. Such a committee may also feel that it is susceptible to administrative use as a shield for unpopular decisions (M. E. Brown in "Four Issues" 1982, pp. 7A–8A).

Possible initiatives for increasing the intrinsic satisfactions for faculty in participating in institutional decision making relate to setting terms of service on committees to fit better with committee work assignments, providing a proper time perspective for decision making, and providing a better understanding of the political dynamics of decision making. Dissatisfactions about excessive requests for faculty members to participate are, however, more troublesome.

The standard one-year term for faculty committee assignments makes sense from neither the institution's nor the individual's perspective. When committee terms are one year, the faculty member has little opportunity to identify with the committee assignment and will probably not have the opportunity to complete the task he or she began in the committee (Oldham and Kulik 1983, p. 335). One possible alternative is multiyear terms, which would be especially useful for budget committees where frequent turnover greatly reduces influence and satisfaction for faculty members (R. Meisinger in "Four Issues" 1982, pp. 6A–7A). Another possibility is to give a faculty member a continuing responsibility for a particular substantive committee assignment until that substantive task is completed. Such alternatives give the individual an opportunity to experience a sense of completion and to be able to identify with the finished product (Oldham and Kulik 1983, p. 335).

The time frame for some medium- and long-term planning is frequently confusing to faculty who are relatively unfamiliar with such planning activity. Close administrative attention to working with faculty to increase a sense of time perspective has been noted to greatly reduce faculty frustrations with planning (Ringle and Savickas 1983).

New faculty must be introduced, primarily by other faculty, to the political dynamics of decision making in senates and other institutional forums, to better understand the rules of the game for participation. Inadequate knowledge of those dynamics greatly frustrates the relatively new participant in institutional affairs (Baldridge 1982).

Faculty complaints about excessive requests to participate in institutional decision making as a result of the declining number of eligible participants pose real difficulties for institutional response. These complaints about the heavier service load on the eligible pool are strongest at institutions that have significantly increased the number of temporary and part-time faculty in recent years. ("Four Issues" 1982, pp. 5A–6A). Institutions can do little to respond to these requests short of major modifications in personnel policy, which may be undertaken for broader reasons of qualitative improvement but not solely to reduce the burdens of participation in institutional decision making.

Institutional Rewards

On the whole, the reward system at most institutions of higher education gives little weight to service through participation in institutional decision making. What matters most is what is given greatest weight in discussion of faculty personnel committees, and institutional service is not much discussed by most personnel committees (Tuckman 1976). The standard forms for faculty time expenditure also blur a focus on institutional service by combining it with public service. Although a close relationship does not exist between service (institutional and public service) and faculty salaries, service is rewarded more in some fields than in others. Of the four professional fields Tuckman studied, service was rewarded only in education (Tuckman 1976). The low priority that faculty, especially those in research-

oriented institutions, place upon allotting their own time or colleagues' time for participation (Dykes 1968) underlies the faculty personnel committee behavior Tuckman describes. Some well-established faculty members also express concern about the possibility that institutional service will become an alternate path to career advancement at the expense of scholarly products. In such a perspective, the absence of explicit standards to evaluate the merit of institutional service is especially problemmatic (Lewis 1984).

Some of the most troublesome questions about providing incentives for participation arise with regard to women and minorities, especially at research-oriented universities. A time commitment to committee work at the expense of scholarly accomplishment may endanger the receipt of tenure and progress toward full professional acceptance. Special requests to women and minorities to participate in various aspects of university decision making because of the special perspective they can bring to bear can be inadvertently exploitative if constructive committee participation cannot substitute for some research activity (Weiss 1980).

Higher education institutions must place a high priority on increasing and making explicit the rewards for participation in institutional decision making if they wish to reduce the increasing resistance of some of the institution's most productive faculty to that participation. Special attention also needs to be given to rewarding service to systemwide senates and statewide faculty advisory committees that are less well understood on campus and more personally inconvenient to participants than campus institutional service (Berdahl and Gove 1982).

Faculty participation in institutional decision making is likely to remain a subject of considerable interest. Suggestions for further study involve broad theoretical issues in the development of the literature and specific topics having immediate relevance to practice.

Broad Issues

Refinement of terminology

Higher education scholars should make greater efforts to distinguish between "participation," "power," "influence," and "autonomy," which are frequently used "interchangeably and uncritically in the literature" (Austin and Gamson 1983, p. 35). More needs to be known about the dynamics of faculty influence and power before more refined judgments can be made about the effect of faculty participation in any given situation.

Rationale for participation

Additional applications of generic organization theory to the higher education setting will help further develop the higher education literature on faculty participation in institutional decision making (Bess 1983). Research more explicitly based on concepts widely used in the generic organization theory literature will provide a stronger conceptual base for presentation of the rationale for faculty participation. Such concepts include the relationship between participation and satisfaction, the relationship between satisfaction and individual performance, the quality of work life, and situational requisites for participatory leadership.

A more refined rationale would be a significant contribution to both the theory and the practice of faculty participation. Such a rationale for faculty participation would provide faculty participants in institutional decision making a common reference point for their activity, thus improving communications about the fundamental premises underlying their behavior among themselves, with administrators and other campus constituencies, and with external entities.

Faculty leadership and breadth of faculty vision

The higher education literature does not provide any focused coverage of the leadership role played by faculty serving in roles like chair of the campuswide academic senate or chair of a committee directly advisory to a president or academic vice president. Both the interactions between faculty leaders and other faculty participants and the interactions between faculty leaders and administrative leaders should be examined. It is likely that rather major modifications will be necessary to apply generic organization theory to such faculty leadership, which has no direct parallel in business or other organizational settings.

Strengthening institutional perceptions that faculty are orienting themselves to a broad set of interests and have a strong concern about the overall health of the institution is central to limiting institutional resistance to faculty participation (Baldridge 1982). Given the relative narrowness of the faculty vision on some matters, such as general education and staffing flexibility, more needs to be known about the dynamic for formation and evolution of the faculty vision. Faculty and administrators will find such insights useful when seeking faculty participants' adoption of a broad rather than a narrow outlook in any given decision.

Organizational and political dynamics

Although recent higher education literature recognizes more fully the significance of the organizational and political dynamics of decision making than did the earlier literature, it still does not address a very broad range of potential organizational and political factors. Further insight therefore needs to be provided on patterns of conflict and consensus, on informal decision making, and on shifts in political dynamics. Special attention might also be given to the politics of faculty participation in the budgetary process, which can draw upon a rich literature on budgeting dynamics in other types of organizations (Wildavsky 1975).

Approaches for improving administrative leadership

Higher education scholars should give more attention to two aspects of administrative leadership in higher education: selection and training of administrators in participatory leadership skills and administrative approaches to institutional renewal and transformation.

A sizable generic organization theory literature based on relatively well-developed organizational process in some business organizations includes approaches for selection and training to improve participatory leadership skills (Yukl 1981, pp. 278–85). By contrast, both institutional practice and the higher education literature are somewhat underdeveloped in those areas, especially in training and development. The literature on administrative selection in higher education has grown significantly in recent years but reflects significant differences about how to ensure that the candidate selected has the desirable behavioral orientations (Bisesi 1984; Bromert 1984; Maher 1983). Virtually no attention has been given, however, to the training and development of higher education administrators to increase their skills in participatory leadership and in coordinating the consultative process. Administrative style and training and development are likely to be of significant interest in future years, the result not only of an increased interest in issues of participatory leadership but also of the adoption of faculty collective bargaining on a number of campuses (Baldridge, Kemerer, and associates 1981, pp. 15, 18). More research is needed on how to handle factors of participatory orientation and skills in the processes of selection and of training and development for higher education administrators.

The literature on transformational leadership (that is, leadership that emphasizes shared values and goals) should be further developed on the basis of extended examination of higher education institutions and other organizations (Vroom 1983). Conditions that promote the emergence of transformational leaders and methods to facilitate that emergence should be examined (Bass 1981, pp. 609–11). The methods by which a transformational leader moves organizational constituencies away from a defensive response to threats, gets them to come to terms fully with the threat, and moves them toward consensus on an overarching set of institutional goals also requires further examination (Bass 1981, pp. 609–10).

Institutional differences in patterns of participation
Much of the literature on faculty participation examines the experience at major research universities; a relatively small portion examines patterns at other types of institu-

Virtually no attention has been given, however, to the training and development of higher education administrators to increase their skills in participatory leadership. . . .

tions. As a result, the literature provides greatest coverage of those institutions where faculty participation is the most well established but also where the problems of institutional rewards for participation are most severe. More research should focus on patterns of participation at types of institutions other than research universities. Such research should help illuminate differences between institutions and the source of those differences.

Specific Topical Areas

Certain topical areas deserve priority attention for research, and the results of research in those areas should be made available to faculty and administrators who are involved in campuswide consultative processes. The presentation of research results might take the form of a manual or a guidebook that is easily comprehensible to individuals who are already overloaded with important reading material. Several first-generation manuals are available (see Sashkin 1982 for a manual for the business community and Newman and Mortimer 1985 and Powers and Powers 1983 for manuals for the higher education community).

Some topical areas for research that parallel a number of the main chapters of this monograph are suggested in the following paragraphs. Research on such topics is a significant part of working toward the further development and refinement of the process and procedures of faculty participation in institutional decision making.

Academic senates
1. To what extent have academic senates during the 1980s become more representative of institutional faculty through democratizing procedures for committee selection and operation?
2. What are the advantages and disadvantages of various mechanisms and approaches for ensuring that academic senates serve to express a faculty point of view while still recognizing the perspectives of other campus constituencies?
3. What approaches are used to balance consensual and majority approaches to decision making on campuses where the academic senate is influential and well respected?

4. What evolution of relationship between academic senates and collective bargaining agents is occurring on those campuses where collective bargaining has existed for at least 10 years and where the scope of bargaining has tended to broaden?
5. What refinements can be made in criteria for evaluating the effectiveness of academic senates?

Participation by functional area

1. What are the patterns of success and failure at various institutions with regard to faculty participation in the following functional areas:
   - Curriculum—experiences in revising and strengthening general education and other core requirements?
   - Personnel—tenure and staffing flexibility; faculty codes of conduct?
   - Administrative selection and evaluation—evaluation of participatory orientation and skills of candidates; evaluation of internal candidates in presidential searches?
   - Budgeting—direct involvement of faculty at significant decision points?
   - Retrenchment and financial exigency—development of priorities during a period of retrenchment; development and implementation of procedures for financial exigency?
2. What are the positive and negative effects of the following administrative approaches to planning upon opportunities for and effectiveness of faculty participation?
   - Formal democratic planning?
   - Incentive planning?
   - Strategic planning?

Participation at the system and state levels

1. What are the opportunities and obstacles to the establishment of systemwide senates or statewide advisory committees where they do not already exist?
2. What are some of the tradeoffs that faculty face in determining the appropriate substantive stance to take as participants in senates or committees at the system and state levels?

3. To what extent do systemwide senates represent faculty? To what extent have the procedures for selecting committees been democratized?
4. What is the effect of collective bargaining on the functioning of systemwide academic senates? How has the relationship between systemwide senates and collective bargaining agents evolved where collective bargaining has existed at least 10 years and where the scope of bargaining has tended to broaden?
5. What are appropriate refinements in criteria for evaluating the effectiveness of systemwide senates and statewide advisory committees?

Strengthening consultative processes
1. What are the most significant differences between successful and unsuccessful attempts to rebuild collegial foundations for decision making? What specific steps are necessary to implement the revised approach to rebuilding shared values and goals in the undergraduate curriculum as suggested by a number of blue ribbon study committees? What are the specific advantages and disadvantages of using Theory Z and other Japanese management approaches as a way to focus attention on administrative styles consistent with collegially oriented decision making?
2. Through what means have nationally prominent higher education administrators with strong reputations for a participatory orientation learned their skills in leading participatory decision making?
3. Through what means have chairs of academic senates (and other faculty who regularly play a coordinating role relative to faculty participation) who are regarded as successful leaders learned their skills in leading faculty in participatory decision making?
4. What opportunities for training and development exist for faculty members and for administrators who wish to increase their skills in managing and engaging in consultative processes? What are the strengths and weaknesses of the various available opportunities for training and development? What incentives and disincentives exist for faculty and administrators who wish to avail themselves of such opportunities?

5. What are the opportunities for and obstacles to sharing leadership in decision-making groups involving administrators and faculty?
6. What are some administrative techniques that have been successfully employed in avoiding hasty decisions, incomplete participation, and superficial action in decision-making groups?

Increasing faculty satisfaction with participation

1. By what means have those faculty members who are most satisfied with their participation in institutional decision making learned the dynamics of the participatory process? What sources of intrinsic satisfaction and institutional reward do they identify?
2. What additional means are institutions adopting in the late 1980s to increase the intrinsic satisfactions of and institutional rewards for faculty participation?
3. How do current patterns of institutional rewards for participation vary by institutional type? Does the impact of strategies to increase intrinsic satisfactions or institutional rewards vary by institutional type?
4. What approaches have institutions used to moderate pressures on minorities and women to participate in a large number of committees or to reduce personnel system penalties for that participation?

REFERENCES

The ERIC Clearinghouse on Higher Education abstracts and indexes the current literature on higher education for the National Institute of Education's monthly bibliographic journal, *Resources in Education*. Most of these publications are available through the ERIC Document Reproduction Service (EDRS). For publications cited in this bibliography that are available from EDRS, ordering number and price are included. Readers who wish to order a publication should write to ERIC Document Reproduction Service, 3900 Wheeler Avenue, Alexandria, Virginia 22304. When ordering, please specify the document number. Documents are available as noted in microfiche (MF) and paper copy (PC). Because prices are subject to change, it is advisable to check the latest issue of *Resources in Education* for current cost based on the number of pages in the publication.

American Association for Higher Education. 1967. *Faculty Participation in Academic Governance*. Washington, D.C.: National Education Association.

American Association of University Professors. May/June 1984. "Statewide Boards of Higher Education: The Faculty Role." *Academe* 70: 16a.

American Association of University Professors/American Council on Education/Association of Governing Boards. 1966. "Statement on Government of Colleges and Universities." *AAUP Bulletin* 52: 375–79.

Anderson, Richard E. 1983. *Finance and Effectiveness: A Study of College Environments*. Princeton, N.J.: Educational Testing Service.

Andrew, Loyd D. February 1979. "Involving Faculty in Planning." *Planning for Higher Education* 7: 27–31.

Angell, George W. May/June 1978. "Management Prerogatives and Faculty Rights." *Journal of Higher Education* 49: 77–92.

Armijo, Frank; Hall, Richard S.; Lenning, Oscar T.; Jonas, Stephen; Cherin, Ellen; and Harrington, Charles. 1980. *Comprehensive Institutional Planning: Studies in Implementation*. Boulder, Colo.: National Center for Higher Education Management Systems. ED 195 221. pp. MF–$0.97; PC not available EDRS.

Arns, Robert G., and Poland, William. May/June 1980. "Changing the University through Program Review." *Journal of Higher Education* 51: 268–84.

Assembly on University Goals and Governance. 1971. *A First Report*. Cambridge, Mass. Harvard University, American Academy of Arts and Sciences.

Austin, Ann E., and Gamson, Zelda F. 1983. *Academic Workplace: New Demands, Heightened Tensions*. ASHE-ERIC Higher Education Research Report No. 10. Washington, D.C.: Association for the Study of Higher Education. ED 243 397. 131 pp. MF–$0.97; PC–$12.96.

Balderston, Frederick E. 1974. *Managing Today's University*. San Francisco: Jossey-Bass.

Baldridge, J. Victor. January/February 1982. "Shared Governance: A Fable about the Lost Magic Kingdom." *Academe* 68: 12–15.

Baldridge, J. Victor; Curtis, David V.; Ecker, George; and Riley, Gary L. 1978. *Policy Making and Effective Leadership*. San Francisco: Jossey-Bass.

Baldridge, J. Victor; Kemerer, Frank R.; and associates. 1981. *Assessing the Impact of Faculty Collective Bargaining*. AAHE-ERIC Higher Education Research Report No. 8. Washington, D.C.: American Association for Higher Education. ED 216 653. 66 pp. MF–$0.97; PC–$7.14.

Baldridge, J. Victor, and Okimi, Patricia H. October 1982. "Strategic Planning in Higher Education: New Tool—or New Gimmick?" *AAHE Bulletin* 35: 6 + .

Baldridge, J. Victor, and Tierney, Michael L. 1979. *New Approaches to Management*. San Francisco: Jossey-Bass.

Barak, Robert J. 1982. *Program Review in Higher Education: Within and Without*. Boulder, Colo.: National Center for Higher Education Management Systems.ED 246 829. 137 pp. MF–$0.97; PC–$12.96.

Bass, Bernard M. 1981. *Stogdill's Handbook of Leadership*. Rev. and expanded ed. New York: Free Press.

Begin, James P. May/June 1978. "Statutory Definitions of the Scope of Negotiations: The Implications for Traditional Faculty Governance." *Journal of Higher Education* 49: 247–60.

Benjamin, Ernest. September/October 1985. "Expanding the Context of Curriculum Reform." *Academe* 71: 28–31.

Berdahl, Robert O., and Gove, Samuel K. May/June 1982. "Governing Higher Education: Faculty Roles on State Boards." *Academe* 68: 21–24.

Bess, James L. Summer 1983. "Maps and Gaps in the Study of College and University Organization." *Review of Higher Education* 6: 239–52.

Bisesi, Michael. April 1984. "Assessing Candidates: Better Ways for the Best Results." *AAHE Bulletin* 36: 11–13.

Bobbitt, H. Randolph, Jr., and Behling, Orlando C. January/February 1981. *Journal of Higher Education* 52: 29–44.

Bowen, Howard R., and Schuster, Jack H. Forthcoming. *American Professors: A National Resource Imperiled.* New York: Oxford University Press.

Bradford, Leland P., ed. 1976. *Group Development.* 2d ed. La Jolla, Calif.: University Associates.

Bromert, Jane Doyle. April 1984. "The Role and Effectiveness of Search Committees." *AAHE Bulletin* 36: 7–10. ED 243 355. 5 pp. MF–$0.97; PC–$3.54.

Brown, J. Douglas. 1977. "Departmental and University Leadership." In *Academic Departments: Problems, Variations, and Alternatives,* edited by Dean E. McHenry. San Francisco: Jossey-Bass.

Burns, James MacGregor. 1978. *Leadership.* New York: Harper & Row.

Carnegie Commission on Higher Education. 1973. *Governance of Higher Education: Six Priority Problems.* New York: McGraw-Hill.

Carnegie Council on Policy Studies in Higher Education. 1977. *Faculty Bargaining in Public Higher Education.* San Francisco: Jossey-Bass.

Caruthers, J. Kent, and Lott, Gary B. 1981. *Mission Review: Foundation for Strategic Planning.* Boulder, Colo.: National Center for Higher Education Management Systems. ED 208 757. 188 pp. MF–$0.97; PC–$16.97.

Chaffee, Ellen Earle. October 1981. *On Deciding How to Decide: To Centralize or Decentralize.* Occasional paper. Boulder, Colo.: National Center for Higher Education Management Systems.

———. 1983. *Rational Decision Making in Higher Education.* Boulder, Colo.: National Center for Higher Education Management Systems.

Chait, Richard P. March/April 1982a. "Look Who Invented Japanese Management." *AGB Reports* 24: 3–7.

———. July/August 1982b. "Response to David Nichols." *AGB Reports* 24: 13–14.

Clark, Burton R. 1968. "The New University." In *The State of the University,* edited by Carlos E. Kruytbosch and Sheldon L. Messinger. Beverly Hills, Calif.: Sage Publications.

Clark, Carlene A. September/October 1981. "The Yeshiva Case: An Analysis of Its Potential Impact on Public Universities." *Journal of Higher Education* 52: 449–69.

Coch, L., and French, J.R.P., Jr. 1948. "Overcoming Resistance to Change." *Human Relations* 1: 512–32.

Cohen, Michael D., and March, James G. 1974. *Leadership and Ambiguity: The American College President*. New York: McGraw-Hill.

Commission on Academic Tenure in Higher Education. 1973. *Faculty Tenure*. San Francisco: Jossey-Bass.

Commission on Strengthening Presidential Leadership. 1984. *Presidents Make a Difference: Strengthening Leadership in Colleges and Universities*. Washington, D.C.: Association of Governing Boards. ED 247 879. 140 pp. MF–$0.97; PC not available EDRS.

Cope, Robert G. October 1972. "Bases of Power, Administrative Preferences, and Job Satisfaction: A Situational Approach." *Journal of Vocational Behavior* 2: 457–65.

———. 1981. *Strategic Planning, Management, and Decision Making*. AAHE-ERIC Higher Education Research Report No. 9. Washington, D.C.: American Association for Higher Education. ED 217 825. 75 pp. MF–$0.97; PC–$7.14.

Corson, John J. 1960. *Governance of Colleges and Universities*. New York: McGraw-Hill.

Cummings, Thomas G., and Molloy, Edmond S. 1977. *Improving Productivity and the Quality of Work Life*. New York: Praeger.

Cyert, Richard M. 1980. "Managing Universities in the 1980s." In *Essays on Higher Education,* edited by Chris Argyris and Richard M. Cyert. Cambridge, Mass.: Harvard University, Institute for Educational Management.

Deegan, William L., and Mortimer, Kenneth P. 1970. *Faculty in Governance at the University of Minnesota*. Berkeley, Calif.: University of California, Center for Research and Development in Higher Education. ED 042 435. 64 pp. MF–$0.97; PC–$7.14.

"A Dialogue on the Structure of Governance." September/October 1983. *AGB Reports* 25: 8–13.

Dill, David. 1971. *Case Studies in University Governance*. Washington, D.C.: National Association of State Universities and Land-Grant Colleges.

Dykes, Archie B. 1968. *Faculty Participation in Academic Decision Making*. Washington, D.C.: American Council on Education.

Epstein, Leon D. 1974. *Governing the University: The Campus and the Public Interest*. San Francisco: Jossey-Bass.

"Faculty Governance in the 1980s: Adverse Conditions, Diverse Responses." December 1981. *Academe* 67: 383–86.

Farmer, Charles H. June 1978. "The Faculty Role in Administrator Evaluation." In *Developing and Evaluating Administrative Leadership,* edited by Charles F. Fisher. New Directions for Higher Education No. 22. San Francisco: Jossey-Bass.

Fiedler, Fred E. 1967. *A Theory of Leadership Effectiveness.*
New York: McGraw-Hill.

Field, R.H. George. April 1979. "A Critique of the Vroom-Yetton
Contingency Model of Leadership Behavior." *Academy of
Management Review* 4: 249–57.

―――. 1982. "A Test of the Vroom-Yetton Normative Model of
Leadership." *Applied Psychology* 67: 523–32.

Finkelstein, Martin J. 1984. *The American Academic Profession:
A Synthesis of Social Scientific Inquiry since World War II.*
Columbus: Ohio State University Press.

Finkelstein, Martin J., and Pfinister, Allan O. 1984. "The Dimin-
ishing Role of Faculty in Institutional Governance: Liberal Arts
Colleges as the Negative Case." Paper presented at the annual
meeting of the Association for the Study of Higher Education.
March, Chicago, Illinois. ED 245 611. 18 pp. MF–$0.97; PC–
$3.54.

Floyd, Carol Everly. 1982. *State Planning, Budgeting, and
Accountability: Approaches for Higher Education.* AAHE-
ERIC Research Report No. 6. Washington, D.C.: American
Association for Higher Education. ED 224 452. 58 pp. MF–
$0.97; PC–$7.14.

Folger, John K. 1980. "Implications of State Government
Changes." In *Improving Academic Management,* edited by
Paul Jedamus and Marvin W. Peterson. San Francisco: Jossey-
Bass.

Foote, Caleb; Mayer, Henry; and associates. 1968. *The Culture
of the University: Governance and Education.* San Francisco:
Jossey-Bass.

Fortunato, Ray T., and Waddell, D. Geneva. 1981. *Personnel
Administration in Higher Education.* San Francisco: Jossey-
Bass.

"Four Issues in Contemporary Campus Governance." January/
February 1982. *Academe* 68: 3A–14A.

Furniss, W. Todd. Spring 1977. "The 1976 AAUP Retrenchment
Policy." *Educational Record* 57: 133–39.

"The Future." January/February 1982. *Academe* 68: 13A–14A.

Garbarino, Joseph W. 1975. *Faculty Bargaining: Change and
Conflict.* New York: McGraw-Hill.

Gove, Samuel K., and Floyd, Carol E. January/February 1975.
"Research on Higher Education Administration and Policy: An
Uneven Report." *Public Administration Review* 35: 111–18.

Groves, Roderick T. June 1977. "Guidelines for Emergency."
AGB Reports 19: 39–46.

————. Fall 1981. "Change, Cohesion, and Tenure Policy: An Illinois Experience with Staffing Plans." *Planning for Higher Education* 10: 9–15.

Haas, Raymond M. 1980. "Acceptance for Institutional Research and Planning." In *Improving Academic Management,* edited by Paul Jedamus and Marvin W. Peterson. San Francisco: Jossey-Bass.

Hammond, Martine F., and Tompkins, Loren D. 1983. "A Major University's Response to a Mandated Budget Recision." Paper presented at the annual meeting of the Association for the Study of Higher Education, March, Washington, D.C.

Helsabeck, Robert E. 1973. *The Compound System.* Berkeley: University of California, Center for Research and Development in Higher Education.

Hersey, Paul, and Blanchard, Kenneth H. 1977. *Management of Organizational Behavior.* 3d ed. Englewood Cliffs, N.J.: Prentice-Hall.

Heydinger, Richard B. 1980. "Academic Program Planning Reconsidered." In *Academic Planning for the 1980s,* edited by Richard B. Heydinger. New Directions for Institutional Research No. 28. San Francisco: Jossey-Bass.

Hines, Edward R., and Hartmark, Leif F. 1980. *Politics of Higher Education.* AAHE-ERIC Higher Education Research Report No. 7. Washington, D.C.: American Association For Higher Education. ED 201 263. 85 pp. MF–$0.97; PC–$9.36.

Hodgkinson, Harold L. 1974. *The Campus Senate: Experiment in Campus Democracy.* Berkeley: University of California, Center for Research and Development in Higher Education.

Holt, Larry C., and Wagner, Thomas E. Spring 1983. "Quality Circles: An Alternative for Higher Education." *Journal of the College and University Personnel Association* 34: 11–14.

House, Robert J. September 1971. "A Path Goal Theory of Leader Effectiveness." *Administrative Science Quarterly* 16: 321–39.

Jacobson, Robert L. 9 May 1984. "When Faculty Cuts Also Cut into 'Shared Governance.' " *Chronicle of Higher Education* 24: 23, 25.

Johnson, Annette B. July 1981. "The Problem of Contraction: Legal Considerations in University Retrenchment." *Journal of Law and Education* 10: 269–324.

Johnson, Mark D., and Mortimer, Kenneth P. 1977. *Faculty Bargaining and the Politics of Retrenchment in the Pennsylvania State Colleges, 1971–1976.* University Park: Pennsylvania State University, Center for the Study of Higher Education. ED 148 201. 112 pp. MF–$0.97; PC–$11.16.

Johnstone, Ronald L. 1981. *The Scope of Faculty Collective Bargaining.* Westport, Conn.: Greenwood.

Kamber, Richard. 12 December 1984. "Dissatisfied Professors and the Erosion of Shared Governance." *Chronicle of Higher Education* 29: 96.

Kanter, Rosabeth. 1983. *The Change Masters: Innovation for Productivity in the American Corporation.* New York: Simon & Schuster.

Keeton, Morris. 1971. *Shared Authority on Campus.* Washington, D.C.: American Association for Higher Education.

Keller, George. 1983. *Academic Strategy: The Management Revolution in American Higher Education.* Baltimore: Johns Hopkins.

Kemerer, Frank R., and Baldridge, J. Victor. May/June 1981. "Senates and Unions: Unexpected Peaceful Coexistence." *Journal of Higher Education* 52: 256–64.

Kerr, Clark. September 1984. "Liberal Learning: A Record of Presidential Neglect." *Change* 16: 32–36.

Kieft, Raymond N. 1978. *Academic Planning: Four Institutional Case Studies.* Boulder, Colo.: National Center for Higher Education Management Systems. ED 154 713. 152 pp. MF–$.097; PC–$15.17.

Kieft, Raymond N.; Armijo, Frank; and Bucklew, Neil. 1978. *A Handbook for Institutional Academic and Program Planning.* Boulder, Colo.: National Center for Higher Education Management Systems. ED 161 327. 80 pp. MF–$0.97; PC–$9.36.

Lawler, Edward E., III. 1982. "Education, Management Style, and Organizational Effectiveness." Research sponsored by the National Institute for Education. ED 229 617. 53 pp. MF–$0.97; PC–$7.14.

Lee, Barbara A. 1978. *Collective Bargaining in Four-Year Colleges.* AAHE-ERIC Higher Education Research Report No. 5. Washington, D.C.; American Association for Higher Education. ED 162 542. 85 pp. MF–$0.97; PC–$9.36.

———. Winter 1982. "Contractually Protected Grievance Systems at Unionized Colleges." *Review of Higher Education* 5: 69–85.

Lee, Eugene C., and Bowen, Frank M. 1971. *The Multicampus University: A Study of Academic Governance.* New York: McGraw-Hill.

Levine, Arthur. 1978. *Handbook on Undergraduate Curriculum.* San Francisco: Jossey-Bass.

Lewis, Lionel S. 18 July 1984. "Trying to Define 'Merit' in Academe." *Chronicle of Higher Education* 28: 56.

Locke, Edwin A., and Schweiger, David M. 1979. "Participation in Decision Making: One More Look." *Research in Organizational Behavior* 1: 265–339.

Lowin, Aaron. 1968. "Participative Decision Making: A Model, Literature Critique, and Prescriptions for Research." *Organizational Behavior and Human Performance* 3: 68–106.

McConnell, T. R. 1971. "Faculty Government." In *Power and Authority,* edited by Harold L. Hodgkinson and L. Richard Meeth. San Francisco: Jossey-Bass.

McConnell, T. R., and Edelstein, Stewart. 1977. *Campus Governance at Berkeley: A Study in Jurisdictions.* Berkeley: University of California, Center for Research and Development in Higher Education. ED 138 209. 80 pp. MF–$0.97; PC–$9.36.

McConnell, T. R., and Mortimer, Kenneth P. 1971. *The Faculty in University Governance.* Berkeley: University of California, Center for Research and Development in Higher Education. ED 050 703. 206 pp. MF–$0.97; PC–$18.77.

Maher, Thomas H. May 1983. "Assessing Candidates: There Are Better Ways." *AAHE Bulletin* 35: 12–3 + .

Maier, Norman R. F. 1963. *Problem Solving Discussion and Conferences: Leadership Methods and Skills.* New York: McGraw-Hill.

Marshall, R. Steven. 1976. "Faculty Views of the University's Organizational Legitimacy: A Case Study." ED 139 353. 23 pp. MF–$0.97; PC not available EDRS.

Mason, Henry L. 1972. *College and University Government: A Handbook of Principle and Practice.* New Orleans: Tulane University.

Meisinger, Richard J., and Dubeck, Leroy W. 1984. *College and University Budgeting: An Introduction for Faculty and Academic Administrators.* Washington, D.C.: National Association of College and University Business Officers.

Meyer, Thomas J. 13 February 1985. "U. of Minn. Senate Votes This Week on Plan to Oust Student Members." *Chronicle of Higher Education* 29: 10.

Miller, James L., Jr. Fall 1983. "Strategic Planning as Pragmatic Adaptation." *Planning for Higher Education* 12: 41–47.

Millett, John C. 1978. *New Structures of Campus Power: Success and Failures of Emerging Forms of Institutional Governance.* San Francisco: Jossey-Bass.

Mohr, Lawrence B. 1982. *Explaining Organizational Behavior.* San Francisco: Jossey-Bass.

Moore, Michael A. July/August 1975. "An Experiment in Governance: The Ohio Faculty Senate." *Journal of Higher Education* 46: 365–79.

————. November/December 1978. "On Launching into Exigency Planning." *Journal of Higher Education* 49: 620–38.

Mortimer, Kenneth P.; Bagshaw, Marque; and Masland, Andrew T. 1985. *Flexibility in Academic Staffing: Effective Policies and Practices.* ASHE-ERIC Higher Education Report No. 1. Washington, D.C.: Association for the Study of Higher Education. ED 260 675. 121 pp. MF–$0.97; PC–$11.16.

Mortimer, Kenneth P.; Gunne, Manuel G.; and Leslie, David W. 1976. "Perceived Legitimacy of Decision Making and Academic Governance Patterns in Higher Education." *Research in Higher Education* 4: 273–90.

Mortimer, Kenneth P., and McConnell, T. R. 1978. *Sharing Authority Effectively.* San Francisco: Jossey-Bass.

Mortimer, Kenneth P., and Richardson, Richard C. 1977. *Governance in Institutions with Faculty Unions: Six Case Studies.* University Park: Pennsylvania State University, Center for the Study of Higher Education. ED 140 764. 191 pp. MF–$0.97; PC–$16.97.

Mortimer, Kenneth P., and Tierney, Michael L. 1979. *The Three "R's" of the Eighties: Reduction, Reallocation, and Retrenchment.* AAHE-ERIC Higher Education Research Report No. 4. Washington, D.C.: American Association for Higher Education. ED 172 642. 93 pp. MF–$0.97; PC–$9.36.

Mumper, Michael. May/June 1983. "Faculty and the State Policy Process: The Uses and Limits of Advisory Committees." *Journal of Higher Education* 54: 294–308.

Naisbitt, John. 1982. *Megatrends: Ten New Directions Transforming Our Lives.* New York: Warner Books.

Nason, John W. 1980. *Presidential Assessment: A Challenge to College and University Leadership.* Washington, D.C.: Association of Governing Boards.

————. 1981. "Selecting the Chief Executive." In *Handbook of College and University Trusteeship,* edited by Richard R. Ingram. San Francisco: Jossey-Bass.

Newman, Frank, and Mortimer, Kenneth P. 1985. "The Process of Academic Management: Building Trust and Legitimacy." Manuscript in preparation under the aegis of the American Association for Higher Education.

Nichols, David A. 1 September 1982a. "Can 'Theory Z' Be Applied to Academic Management?" *Chronicle of Higher Education* 24: 72.

————. July/August 1982b. "Challenging Chait on Theory Z." *AGB Reports* 24: 8–14.

Oldham, Greg R., and Kulik, Carol T. Summer 1983. "Motivation Enhancement through Work Redesign." *Review of Higher Education* 6: 323–42.

Olswang, Steven G., and Lee, Barbara A. 1984. *Faculty Freedoms and Institutional Accountability: Interactions and Conflicts.* ASHE-ERIC Higher Education Research Report No. 5. Washington, D.C.: Association for the Study of Higher Education. ED 252 170. 90 pp. MF–$0.97; PC–$9.36.

O'Neil, Robert M. 1971. "Paradoxes of Campus Power." In *New Teaching, New Learning,* edited by G. Kerry Smith. San Francisco: Jossey-Bass.

Ouchi, William G. 1981. *Theory Z.* Reading, Mass.: Addison-Wesley.

Palola, Ernest G.; Lehmann, Timothy; and Blischke, William R. October 1971. "The Reluctant Planner: Faculty in Institutional Planning." *Journal of Higher Education* 42: 587–602.

Pascale, Richard T., and Athos, Anthony G. 1981. *The Art of Japanese Management.* New York: Warner Books.

Perkins, Dennis N. T.; Nieva, Veronica F.; and Lawler, Edward E., III. 1983. *Managing Creation: The Challenge of Building a New Organization.* New York: John Wiley & Sons.

Peters, Thomas J., and Waterman, Robert H., Jr. 1982. *In Search of Excellence: Lessons from America's Best-Run Companies.* New York: Harper & Row.

Pfeffer, Jeffrey. 1978. *Organizational Design.* Arlington Heights, Ill.: AHM Publishing Company.

Pollay, Richard W.; Taylor, Ronald N.; and Thompson, Mark. March/April 1976. "A Model for Horizontal Power Sharing and Participation in University Decision Making." *Journal of Higher Education* 47: 141–57.

Pondrom, Cyrena. December 1981. "Faculty Retrenchment: The Experience of the University of Wisconsin System." In *Coping with Faculty Reduction,* edited by Stephen R. Hample. New Directions for Institutional Research No. 40. San Francisco: Jossey-Bass.

Poulton, Nick L. 1980. "Strategies of Large Universities." In *Improving Academic Management,* edited by Paul Jedamus and Marvin W. Peterson. San Francisco: Jossey-Bass.

Powers, David R., and Powers, Mary F. 1983. *Making Participatory Management Work.* San Francisco: Jossey-Bass.

———. Fall 1984. "How to Orchestrate Participatory Strategic Planning without Sacrificing Momentum." *Educational Record* 65: 48–52.

Project on Redefining the Meaning and Purpose of Baccalaureate Degrees. 1985. *Integrity in the College Curriculum: A Report to the Academic Community*. Washington, D.C.: Association of American Colleges. ED 251 059. 62 pp. MF–$0.97; PC not available EDRS.

Pucik, Vladimir, and Hatvany, Nina. 1983. "Management Practices in Japan and Their Impact on Business Strategy." In *Advances in Strategic Management: A Research Annual,* vol. 1, edited by Robert Lamb. Greenwich, Conn.: JAI Press.

Redinbaugh, L. D., and Redinbaugh, D. F. Winter 1983. "Theory Z Management at Colleges and Universities." *Educational Record* 64: 26–30.

Richardson, Richard C. 1974. "Governance Theory: A Comparison of Approaches." *Journal of Higher Education* 45: 344–54.

Richfield, Jerome. 1971. "Statewide Academic Senate: The Sound and the Fury." In *An Invisible Giant: The California State Colleges,* edited by Donald R. Gerth, James O. Haehn, and associates. San Francisco: Jossey-Bass.

Richman, Barry M., and Farmer, Richard N. 1974. *Leadership, Goals, and Power in Higher Education*. San Francisco: Jossey-Bass.

Ringle, Philip M., and Savickas, Mark L. November/December 1983. "Administrative Leadership: Planning and Time Perspective." *Journal of Higher Education* 54: 649–61.

Robinson, David Z. January/February 1982. "Reflections of a Trustee." *Academe* 68: 6–8.

Sashkin, Marshall. 1982. *A Manager's Guide to Participative Management*. New York: American Management Association.

———. Spring 1984. "Participative Management Is an Ethical Imperative." *Organizational Dynamics* 12: 4–22.

Schuster, Jack H., and Bowen, Harold R. September/October 1985. "The Faculty at Risk." *Change* 17: 12–21.

Smith, Donald K. December 1978. "Faculty Vitality and the Management of University Personnel Policies." In *Evaluating Faculty Performance and Vitality,* edited by Wayne R. Kirschling. New Directions for Institutional Research No. 20. San Francisco: Jossey-Bass.

Smith, Glynton. September/October 1980. "Systematic Information Sharing in Participative University Management." *Journal of Higher Education* 51: 519–26.

Soles, James R. Winter 1973. "Information: Missing Ingredient in University Governance." *Educational Record* 54: 51–55.

Spiro, Louis M., and Campbell, Jill F. 1983. "Higher Education and Japanese Management: Are They Compatible?" Paper presented at the annual forum of the Association for Institutional Research, May, Toronto. ED 232 578. 24 pp. MF–$0.97; PC–$3.54.

Spitzberg, Irving J., Jr. 1980. "Monitoring Social and Political Change." In *Improving Academic Management,* edited by Paul Jedamus and Marvin W. Peterson. San Francisco: Jossey-Bass.

———. September/October 1984. "Governing the Futures of Higher Education: Report of the General Secretary." *Academe* 70: 13a–20a.

Staw, Barry M. Summer 1983. "Motivation Research versus the Art of Faculty Management." *Review of Higher Education* 6: 302–21.

Strohm, Paul. December 1980. "Toward an AAUP Policy on Evaluation of Administrators." *Academe* 66: 406–13.

———. January/February 1983. "Faculty Roles Today and Tomorrow." *Academe* 69: 10–15.

Study Group on the Conditions of Excellence in American Higher Education. 1984. *Involvement in Learning: Realizing the Potential of American Higher Education.* Washington, D.C.: National Institute of Education. ED 246 833. 127 pp. MF–$0.97; PC–$12.96.

Thompson, James D., and Tuden, Arthur. 1974. "Strategies, Structures, and Processes of Organizational Design." In *Organizational Psychology: A Book of Readings,* 2d ed., edited by David A. Kolb, Irwin M. Rubin, and James M. McIntryre. Englewood Cliffs, N.J.: Prentice-Hall.

Touraine, Alan. 1974. *The Academic System in American Society.* New York: McGraw-Hill.

Tucker, Allan. 1981. *Chairing the Academic Department: Leadership among Peers.* Washington, D.C.: American Council on Education.

Tuckman, Harold P. 1976. *Publication, Teaching, and the Academic Reward Structure.* Lexington, Mass.: Lexington Books.

Van Gieson, Nan, and Zirkel, Perry A. Summer 1981. "Fiscal Exit-gency." *Educational Record* 62: 75–77.

Vroom, Victor H. Summer 1983. "Leaders and Leadership in Academe." *Review of Higher Education* 6: 367–86.

Vroom, Victor H., and Yago, Arthur G. 1978. "On the Validity of the Vroom-Yetton Model." *Journal of Applied Psychology.* 63: 151–62.

Vroom, Victor H., and Yetton, Philip W. 1973. *Leadership and Decision Making.* Pittsburgh: University of Pittsburgh Press.

Weisberger, June M. 1978. *Grievance Arbitration in Higher Education: Recent Experience with Arbitration of Faculty Status Disputes*. Washington, D.C.: Academic Collective Bargaining Information Service.

Weiss, Nancy J. Fall 1980. "Participation for Women: In Itself, No Panacea." *Educational Record* 61: 65–67.

White, Lawrence. 1983. "An Analysis of the AAUP's Recommended Institutional Regulation on Financial Exigency." In *Collective Bargaining in a Period of Retrenchment*, edited by Joel M. Douglas. New York: Baruch College, National Center for the Study of Collective Bargaining in Higher Education and the Professions. ED 248 783. 148 pp. MF–$0.97; PC not available EDRS.

Wieland, George F., and Bachman, Jerald G. 1966. "Faculty Satisfaction and the Department Chairmen: A Study of Academic Departments in Twelve Liberal Arts Colleges." Mimeographed. Ann Arbor: University of Michigan, Survey Research Center.

Wildavsky, Aaron. 1975. *Budgeting: A Comparative Theory of Budgetary Processes*. Boston: Little Brown.

Williams, Don; Olswang, Steven G.; and Hargett, Gary. In press. "A Matter of Degree: Faculty Morale as a Function of Involvement in Institutional Decisions during Times of Financial Distress." *Review of Higher Education*.

Wilson, Logan. 1979. *American Academics Then and Now*. New York: Oxford University Press.

Wyer, Jean C. Winter 1982. "Theory Z—The Collegial Model Revisited." *Review of Higher Education* 5: 111–18.

Wynn, Richard, and Guditus, Charles W. 1984. *Team Management: Leadership by Consensus*. Columbus, Ohio: Charles E. Merrill.

Yukl, Gary A. 1981. *Leadership in Organizations*. Englewood Cliffs, N.J.: Prentice-Hall.

Zander, Alvin. 1977. *Groups at Work: Unresolved Issues in the Study of Organizations*. San Francisco: Jossey-Bass.

———. 1982. *Making Groups Effective*. San Francisco: Jossey-Bass.

Zemsky, Robert; Porter, Randall; and Oedel, Laura P. Summer 1978. "Decentralized Planning: To Share Responsibility." *Educational Record* 59: 229–53.

INDEX

Due process, 31

E

Education (discipline): service rewards, 65
Elite colleges: senate influence, 26
Employee participation (see Participation)
Employee productivity, 4
Ethics: professional, 32
Evaluation criteria (program): economic, 35
Expectations, 7
External relations, 13

F

Facilities planning, 13
Fact books, 57
Faculty
     appointment, 31
     conduct, 32
     definition, 20
     information needs, 57–58
     layoff, 29
     leadership, 68
     morale, 7, 9, 39, 53
     new: socialization, 65
     promotion, 21, 31
     recruiting, 30
     relationship with administrators, 54–56
     relationship with system/state-level authorities, 15
     satisfaction, 73
     service load, 65
     student relationship, 32
     tenure, 21
     young, 21, 27
Faculty advisory committees (state level), 43–46, 66
Faculty evaluation, 65–66
Faculty senates (see Academic senates)
Faculty status, 13
Fiedler's contingency model, 3
Financial exigency, 39–41, 71
Financial incentives, 4
Formal democratic planning, 35, 71
Fraud in research, 32

G

General education
     decentralization effect, 49

"Joint Big Decision Committees," 37, 39
Joint participation, 16–17, 51
Junior faculty
        committee membership, 21
        senate membership, 27

K
Keast Commission, 31

L
Leadership
        administrative, 16–17, 68–69
        faculty, 68
        group-centered, 59
        situational theories, 3, 8
        task-oriented, 58–59
        transformational, 69
Liberal arts colleges
        faculty influence, 26
        quality of work life, 9
        senate structure, 20
        shared governance, 15
Liberal arts professoriate, 53
Long range planning, 13

M
Maryland: faculty advisory committees, 44
Meetings: information sources, 58
Merit raises/policy, 7, 30
Minorities
        committee service, 21
        incentives for participation, 66
        senate membership, 27
Models
        contingency leadership, 3
        union/senate interaction, 23
Morale, 7, 9, 39, 53
Multicampus systems, 43

N
National Association of College and University Budget Officers
    (NACUBO), 38
National Center for Higher Education Management Systems, 35
National study commissions, 52, 60
New course approval, 29

New degree program review, 34
New faculty socialization, 65
Newsletters, 58

O
Ohio: campus senate confederation, 44
Organization theory
  centralization vs. decentralization, 47
  literature on, 1
Organizational dynamics, 68
Organizational vitality, 9

P
Part-time faculty, 38
Participation
  employee, 1–6
  faculty right/expectations, 6–7
  incentives, 66
  patterns, 63
  rationale, 67
  research needs, 67–73
  satisfaction, 63–66
  terminology, 67
  types, 11–17
Patent regulations, 32
Peer review, 30, 31
Performance
  generic organization theory, 1–3
  standards: setting, 30
Personnel policy, 32
Personnel status decision making, 30–32
Planning, 34–36, 65, 71
Polarization: group deliberation, 59–60
Policy making
  faculty role, 32
  financial exigency, 41
  planning impact, 34
Policy statements
  academic governance, 13
  faculty personnel status, 32
Political dynamics, 64, 65, 68
Position paper development, 55
Postcrisis inventory, 55
Presidents
  budgetary process, 39
  evaluation, 32

University of Wisconsin at Madison
      town meeting senate, 20
University senates (see Academic senates)

V
Voting, 22
Vroom-Yetton contingency leadership model, 3, 8

W
West Virginia University, 35
Women
      committee service, 21
      incentives for participation, 66
      senate membership, 27
Work environment, 53
Workload, 38, 65

ASHE-ERIC HIGHER EDUCATION REPORTS

Starting in 1983, the Association for the Study of Higher Education assumed cosponsorship of the Higher Education Reports with the ERIC Clearinghouse on Higher Education. For the previous 11 years, ERIC and the American Association for Higher Education prepared and published the reports.

Each report is the definitive analysis of a tough higher education problem, based on a thorough research of pertinent literature and institutional experiences. Report topics, identified by a national survey, are written by noted practitioners and scholars with prepublication manuscript reviews by experts.

Eight monographs (10 monographs before 1985) in the ASHE-ERIC Higher Education Report series are published each year, available individually or by subscription. Subscription to eight issues is $55 regular; $40 for members of AERA, AAHE and AIR: $35 for members of ASHE. (Add $7.50 outside the United States.)

Prices for single copies, including 4th class postage and handling, are $7.50 regular and $6.00 for members of AERA, AAHE, AIR, and ASHE ($6.50 regular and $5.00 for members for reports published before 1983). If faster 1st class postage is desired for U.S. and Canadian orders, add $.75 for each publication ordered: overseas, add $4.50. For VISA and MasterCard payments, include card number, expiration date, and signature. Orders under $25 must be prepaid. Bulk discounts are available on orders of 15 or more reports (not applicable to subscriptions). Order from the Publications Department, Association for the Study of Higher Education, One Dupont Circle, Suite 630, Washington, D.C. 20036, (202/296-2597. Write for a publication list of all the Higher Education Reports available.

1985 Higher Education Reports

1. Flexibility in Academic Staffing: Effective Policies and Practices
   Kenneth P. Mortimer, Marque Bagshaw, and Andrew T. Masland

2. Associations in Action: The Washington, D.C., Higher Education Community
   Harland G. Bloland

3. And on the Seventh Day: Faculty Consulting and Supplemental Income
   Carol M. Boyer and Darrell R. Lewis

4. Faculty Research Performance: Lessons from the Sciences and Social Sciences
   John W. Creswell

5. Academic Program Reviews: Institutional Approaches, Expectations, and Controversies
   Clifton F. Conrad and Richard F. Wilson

6. Students in Urban Settings: Achieving the Baccalaureate Degree
   Richard C. Richardson, Jr., and Louis W. Bender

7. Serving More Than Students: A Critical Need for College Student Personnel Services
   Peter H. Garland

---

8. Faculty Participation in Decision Making: Necessity or Luxury?
   Carol E. Floyd

1984 Higher Education Reports

1. Adult Learning: State Policies and Institutional Practices
   K. Patricia Cross and Anne-Marie McCartan

2. Student Stress: Effects and Solutions
   Neal A. Whitman, David C. Spendlove, and Claire H. Clark

3. Part-time Faculty: Higher Education at a Crossroads
   Judith M. Gappa

4. Sex Discrimination Law in Higher Education: The Lessons of the Past Decade
   J. Ralph Lindgren, Patti T. Ota, Perry A. Zirkel, and Nan Van Gieson

5. Faculty Freedoms and Institutional Accountability: Interactions and Conflicts
   Steven G. Olswang and Barbara A. Lee

6. The High-Technology Connection: Academic Industrial Cooperation for Economic Growth
   Lynn G. Johnson

7. Employee Educational Programs: Implications for Industry and Higher Education
   Suzanne W. Morse

8. Academic Libraries: The Changing Knowledge Centers of Colleges and Universities
   Barbara B. Moran

9. Futures Research and the Strategic Planning Process: Implications for Higher Education
   James L. Morrison, William L. Renfro, and Wayne I. Boucher

10. Faculty Workload: Research, Theory, and Interpretation
    Harold E. Yuker

1983 Higher Education Reports

1. The Path to Excellence: Quality Assurance in Higher Education
   Laurence R. Marcus, Anita O. Leone, and Edward D. Goldberg

2. Faculty Recruitment, Retention, and Fair Employment: Obligations and Opportunities
   John S. Waggaman

3. Meeting the Challenges: Developing Faculty Careers
   Michael C. T. Brookes and Katherine L. German

4. Raising Academic Standards: A Guide to Learning Improvement
   Ruth Talbott Keimig

5. Serving Learners at a Distance: A Guide to Program Practices
   Charles E. Feasley

Yes, I want to receive the other 7 reports in the 1985 ASHE-ERIC Higher Education Report series at the special discount price. I have just bought Report No. ___ at $7.50. Please deduct this amount from the price of my subscription.

ORDER FORM

Association for the Study of Higher Education
One Dupont Circle, Suite 630
Washington, D.C. 20036
Phone: (202) 296-2597

Name _____

Position _____

Inst./Address _____

_____

_____

Day Phone _____

Signature _____

☐ Check enclosed (payable to ASHE)
☐ Purchase order attached
☐ Charge my VISA account

_____

Exp. date _____

☐ Charge my MasterCard account

_____

Exp. date _____

Type	Subscription	This issue	TOTAL
Regular	$55.00	– $7.50	$47.50
AERA, AIR, AAHE member	$40.00	– $7.50	$32.50
ASHE member	$35.00	– $7.50	$27.50

". . . A valuable series, especially for reviewing and revising academic programs. These reports can save us all from pitfalls and frustrations."

Mark H. Curtis, former President
Association of American Colleges

Dear Librarian,

I have just finished reading one of the 1985 ASHE-ERIC Higher Education Reports (ISSN 0884-0040). I found it outstanding and strongly recommend that our institution subscribe to the series. At $55.00 for 8 issues, it is a bargain.

Signed,

Name _____

Title _____

Association for the Study of Higher Education
The George Washington University
One Dupont Circle, Suite 630, Dept. 51
Washington, D.C. 20036
Phone: (202) 296-2597

ORDER FORM

No.   Amount

____ 1985 Series $55.00   _____

____ 1986 Series $55.00   _____

____ Please place a standing order(s) for this institution @ $55.00/yr.   _____

       TOTAL DUE: _____

Name _____

Position _____

Inst./Address _____

_____

_____

Day Phone _____

Signature _____

☐ Check enclosed (payable to ASHE)
☐ Purchase order attached

FROM: _____
_____
_____
_____

Association for the Study of Higher Education
Attention: Subscription Department
One Dupont Circle, Suite 630
Washington, DC 20036

FROM: _____
_____
_____
_____

ATTN: Serial Acquisitions Dept.
The Library

_____
_____
_____